PINING WIND

A Cycle of Nō Plays

(The first of two volumes)

Translated by Royall Tyler

East Asia Program
Cornell University
Ithaca, New York 14853

© Royall Tyler 1978
Seventh printing 1992
ISSN 8756-5293
ISBN 0-939657-17-1

TABLE OF CONTENTS

INTRODUCTION

My work on these two volumes began, although I was far from realizing it at the time, when in one of Donald Keene's classes at Columbia I first read Matsukaze ("Pining Wind"). The play was so difficult that in the end I had no idea what I had just struggled through, and could remember nothing about it. And yet it had moved me deeply. I felt Matsukaze demanded expert translation, but at the same time it seemed untranslatable because of the very word plays that help make it so effective. Therefore I gave up the idea immediately.

A few years later Donald Keene kindly asked me to write introductions for the plays in Twenty Plays of the Nō Theater which he was then preparing for publication. Soon I found myself unable to resist editing and correcting as well; and among the manuscripts which I examined was a translation of Matsukaze. I was glad to see that someone had attempted what was still to my mind impossible, but I was suddenly possessed by the urge to do better. Therefore I rashly plunged into translating Matsukaze myself, after all. The result was the version which eventually appeared in the book.

Though pleased at first, I shortly took to feeling that I had not yet really translated Matsukaze at all. It seemed inevitable that I would try again when the time was right. The right time did come a few more years later in a remote village in New Mexico. As I recall I translated Nue ("Nightbird") first, then Matsukaze, then Eguchi ("Mouth-of Sound"). The desert was so grand, and so utterly different from

1

Japan, that the moonlit shore of Suma came most vividly alive by contrast in my imagination.

Thanks to Andrea Miller of the Asia Society, a Boston publisher eventually expressed interest in my translations and encouraged me to do a book. The maximum manuscript size which he mentioned seemed to allow more nō and kyōgen translations than I had ever expected to do, and I promptly drew up an outline which filled the maximum almost to overflowing. In 1975, however, when the manuscript was ready and even edited, financial difficulties forced the publisher to abandon the project.

Rereading my work now, or remembering it, I recognize many flaws. There are lapses in quality, genuine obscurities, unsuccessful experiments, and of course mistakes. My imperfect mastery of my own language has left many rough edges and surfaces. In a word, I have been tempted to go over the whole thing again. But I have not done so. For I do take pride in these translations and believe that some of them contain genuine poetry. I have the greatest reservations, I think, about my version of Kinuta ("The Block"). I did not appreciate this extraordinary play when I worked on it, and I will doubtless retranslate it in the future.

One person who read my new Matsukaze commented that my first translation was far kinder to the reader. I agree. However, my intention was not to be kind to the reader, but to transcribe the texture of the Japanese. And the Japanese is anything but kind to the reader. Surely it does not matter much whether one is Japanese, medieval or modern, or American: a play like Matsukaze is full of difficult poetry. Hart Crane too (a native of Ohio, the state where I now teach, and a magnificent poet) wrote verse of such difficulty that a translator too concerned with kindness to the reader could hardly represent him fairly in another language. Of more urgent concern are density, resonance, and music. These are qualities of nō language which impress me greatly, and it is for them that I have reached.

It seems to me that people used to wonder how Zeami's audiences could possibly understand the best passages of nō. The truly sophisticated listener might "get" the allusions and the double meanings, but what of the lesser man? How could he make any sense of the proceedings? By now, however, I believe that nobody, whether courtier or peasant, understood such poetry analytically. What the audience "got," with more or less refinement of detail according to sensitivity and education, was emotion. In other words, I take a nō play to be, linguistically and otherwise, an elaborate device designed to convey pure feeling. No ingenuity in nō should be of any value unless it enhances the play's dominant emotional tone. And once that tone is powerfully experienced, all the complexities of nō are like the raft of the Teaching with which the Buddhist disciple is reminded not to weigh himself down after it has borne him to the Other Shore.

Here I would like to refer again to Hart Crane whose poetry I keep rereading for its splendid sound and power despite many passages which analytically I hardly understand at all. As a biographer put it, for Crane "The total poem defines a feeling in exactly the way a word defines a concept." And the same biographer quoted Crane as follows: "It is as though a poem gave the reader as he left it a single, new word, never before spoken and impossible to actually enunciate." This

"word," as the context makes clear, is an emotion. Crane then went
on to say, "The terms of expression employed are often selected less
for their logical (literal) significance than for their associational
meanings. Via this and their metaphorical relationships, the entire
construction of the poem is raised on the organic principle of a
'logic of metaphor . . .'"*

These remarks, I believe, apply beautifully to nō, illuminating
it both as poetry and as dramatic event. Zeami was clearly a great
master of the "logic of metaphor." But it is true that he did not
know that he was. He did not need to. The tradition already supplied
him with just that orientation toward his art, and a great wealth of
material with which to weave his own potent designs. And yet for us
fully to understand nō, we must have the sort of awareness which Crane
achieved for himself toward his own work; achieved because in a frag-
mented world without coherent tradition he needed to define abstractly
just what it was that he was doing.

Therefore if we wish to understand as well as to experience the
fascination of nō, we, unlike Zeami, must consciously study meaning.
Zeami did not discuss meaning because, with his and his culture's sure
sense of the fittingness of things, he could take it for granted. But
his "logic of metaphor," though to him perhaps inevitable, is foreign
to us. Being from another place and time, we ask why. Why does
Murasame (Sudden Rain in the present Matsukaze) not remember Yukihira's

---

* John Unterecker. Voyager: A Life of Hart Crane. New York, Farrar,
Straus and Giroux, 1969, pp. 377-378. The quotations from Crane are
from an essay entitled "General Aims and Theories."

promise? What does the Emperor's lost hawk, in _Nomori_ ("The Watchman's Mirror") have to do with the play? Why does a mad _shite_ wear her robe off one shoulder? And why is the onset of madness (as in _Hanjo_, not translated here) associated with the falling of the first autumn leaf? There are endless questions like these. Documentary research cannot fully answer them. What is required is the informed imagination. And (to touch again upon the question of style) the imagination cannot be well informed if a translation does not transcribe the logic of nō metaphor as clearly as possible. Certainly the translator, at least, must imaginatively comprehend what he is translating.

An example from _Eguchi_ will illustrate the problem. In _Eguchi_ Kan'ami associates the Lady's boat, and the Lady herself therefore, with the moon. He does not say that the Lady is the moon but he pervasively suggests as much. The mind's eye sees her between her two attendants, robed in all the colors of love, sailing the broad stream in a flood of moonlight; and the ear hears her preaching the very truth of the sorrow of human existence. Between her and the moon there must be a profound connection. And indeed the poetry, linking nouns as it does without specifying in any way the relationship between them, confirms the vision. Yet a translation into plain English (or into modern standard Japanese) cannot preserve this association because grammar forbids it. Once the translator has seen such things, however, he cannot but wish that his reader might see the same.

Thus in translating the poetry of these plays I gave great attention to preserving not grammar (of which there really is often rather little) but image order. It seemed to me that it was the precise

placement of each image which gave the passage its real vitality.
Indeed I easily visualize a passage from nō as a movie sequence full
of elegant dissolves, superimpositions of images, flashes of other
scenes, etc.--all precisely ordered not narratively but associatively.
Therefore I had to render all the puns and pivot words, all the phrases
that go as well with what precedes them as with what follows; all the
extra-grammatical devices which continually fade one line of meaning
into an entirely different one--and sometimes back again. Of course
I often did not succeed, and in some plays I tried less hard than in
others. But I did not find the task impossible. Pivot words and
double meanings of various kinds are not actually alien to English.
Indeed I sometimes found wonderful inventions just begging to be
included, only to have to reject them because they were not in the
original. (Sometimes too, I included a new double meaning if I had
been quite unable to render an original one nearby in the text.)

Perhaps I should give a few examples of these devices. A passage
in my Izutsu ("The Well Cradle") reads,

> Then Mount Tatsuta   aglow with red   leaves
> Ki no Aritsune's daughter   disclosed,   oh shame, as I!

Perhaps the "leaves" here needs no explanation. A little less easy are
these lines from Matsukaze:

> This image shames me   my own form   shrinks low,
> a wain withdrawing tides . . .

The "wain" is the "brine-scoop wagon," but "a wain" also suggests
"away." And the same Matsukaze has a passage (taken actually from the
Tale of Genji) which works the sounds su-ma-no-u-ra (Suma no ura,
"Suma shore") into a phrase which has nothing to do either with Suma

or with shore; and in English I have turned this into:

        I learn no lesson   but ever assume a   surely
        bitter heart!

There is admittedly a problem with such devices in translation,

even if they are successfully handled: they are generally unobtrusive

in Japanese but tend in English to be excessively original. The follow-

ing passage from my Sotoba Komachi ("Komachi on the Gravepost"), for

example, has pivot words in exactly the same places as the Japanese,

and they are really no more difficult to catch. But in English they

certainly are more singular:

        My hundred years lack   wan (one) these hairs
        hankerings (hang) do I   no (know) sooner dawn
        breaks than shame at my looks   covers me.

And this one from Kin'satsu ("The Golden Tablet") is even more tricky:

        A thousand ages   crowd the bamboo staff   joint
        by joint knotted (not at) Fushimi   then are we?

I myself do not understand the reason for the pun and the question; but

there they are. It is necessary in all such cases to hear the sound

of the word while ignoring the spelling, just as in Japanese.

As the above samples show, I have also tried in these translations

a new way of setting out the lines of poetry. Prose in a nō play often

yields only gradually to verse. I reflected that the Japanese way of

writing the text makes it impossible to distinguish at a glance between

verse and prose, and certainly makes it quite unnecessary to worry about

defining the points at which one should begin breaking up the text

into separate lines. Therefore I decided to approximate the Japanese

manner in English. However I did still feel the need for some incon-

spicuous means to set off verse from prose. Perhaps, I thought, the rhetorical devices I had transferred from Japanese to English might then be easier to spot and to understand. As I write now, I am not sure what solution is best, after all. But the run-together method, either partial or total, does save space.

As a glance through these pages will show, I have given a good deal of information about stage movement, style of delivery, and the shōdan, the technical subdivisions of the plays. I claim no special knowledge in these areas, however. I have simply translated almost all such material provided in the pages of the text I used for the nō plays: the two-volume Yōkyoku shū in the Nihon koten bungaku taikei series, edited by Omote Akira and Yokomichi Mario. (Since this edition does not give full information for Hagoromo ("The Feather Mantle") I have not been able to supply it for the translation.) Moreover, the same glance through these pages will reveal another of my experiments: I have translated nearly all technical terms, from waki to yūken, into English. The masks I cite for each play are according to the usage of the Kanze school, since I obtained information on masks from the Yōkyoku taikan edited by Sanari Kentarō.

The introduction I have given each of the nō plays is meant to serve two purposes. First, it provides information essential to an understanding of the play. (Less necessary information is included in a glossary, since there are no footnotes.) Indeed, the material in these introductions is cumulative: I do not discuss the same issue twice even if it is important in more than one play. Second, the introductions interpret meaning. Here, too, the method is cumulative. Once I have outlined a key theme I do not go over it again for a later play. Thus the introductions and their plays are best read in sequence, if possible.

The interpretations I suggest _are_ no more than suggestions. They are incomplete and very little developed. A real commentary on a major nō play might well make a small book. Indeed it might make a large book since there is almost nowhere that reflection on these plays may not take one.

Nō is a genuine "forest of symbols." Not only can one roam through the trees happily and at great length; one can also get lost. Or at least one can discover enchanted glades and lose track of the way home. More plainly speaking, one can discover meanings which seem unrelated either to the play at hand or to the whole Japanese tradition. I have, for example, an implausible idea that the three years Yukihira (in Matsukaze) spent at Suma, his going back up to Miyako, and his death shortly thereafter, are parallel to Christ's ascension to the Father not long after his three days in the tomb. In fact I could support this proposition at some length. However, I am not sure what the parallel may mean even if it is there.

On a less speculative level, though, a great deal more can be done with the interpretation of nō than anyone seems yet to have attempted. Themes recur everywhere: in a phrase, a scene, a play, a group of plays; images echo and enhance one another like bird-calls in a wood. One need go only a very short way in working out a meaning for all these things before one can confidently affirm that Kan'ami, Zeami, etc. "never meant anything of the kind." But the themes and images are there, nonetheless. There the forest is, so to speak, and

the urge to explore can be strong. I know that there are others besides
myself eager to begin.

A grouping of plays thematically related, one which I believe
invites special attention, is the cycle. These two volumes are arranged
according to the prescibed five-play sequence, although since plays of
the third and fourth categories dominate the repertoire, I have ended
up including more than two of each. In addition, the whole collection,
originally meant as it was to make a single volume, is framed by
Hagoromo and Yamamba ("Granny Mountains"). Hagoromo is surely the
basic nō play, both because of its theme and because of the consensus
to that effect of the tradition. Yamamba, on the other hand, is perhaps the most sweeping and vast nō play of all.

To describe briefly my view of the five-play cycle (granted that
all sorts of irregularities could no doubt be found), I see a pattern
like a turning wheel: a wheel which links in one circle heaven and
hell. The god play shows (and therefore creates) ease, freedom, communion between heaven and earth and between all beings, spiritual or
fleshly. In the god play, yume ("dream"; the longings of the spirit)
and utsutsu ("reality"; the solid, diurnal world) are so thoroughly
one that they are not even mentioned. There is no problem. In the
woman play, yume and utsutsu are, alas, quite different from one
another, at least under ordinary circumstances; but the gap can be
bridged by a leap of passion or faith, even if this leap sometimes
resembles madness. Woman plays are in fact about the human realm where
love, in particular, makes us at times so acutely aware of yume and
utsutsu. Then plays of the fourth category introduce a split which

seemingly cannot be resolved under any circumstances. Communion or communication break down totally. In such plays the shite may be completely isolated in a world which to him or her appears undeniably utsutsu whereas we, the onlookers, understand that it is hopelessly yume, a fiction. Finally, the demon play works through the terrible duality and gathers yume and utsutsu again into one.

The five-play cycle therefore has to do with the constant alternation of opposites, in life or in the mind, as the wheel (like the wheels of the brine-scoop wagon or of Hyakuman's cart) turns from high to low yet remains ever the same. This movement is also like the motion of a wave, and the wave is one of the key images in nō. Moreover, if one sees the whole scheme, as the waki (especially in a demon play) is bound to do, one will observe the pattern of human existence as in a mirror--just as the waki does in Nomori. Therefore the mirror, and its close but greater relative, the full, round moon, are equally key images in nō.

So far I have not mentioned the warrior play, which comes second in the program. Warrior plays are a little hard to explain. In any case there are not many of them. But they do perhaps fit in. Unlike the woman who follows him, the warrior is not entirely caught in the world and therefore not deeply involved in a yume at variance with utsutsu. His prime concern is honor, not happiness. And whereas happiness, in nō, depends upon another, honor depends upon the warrior himself. As an honorable man he is true to his highest passion (which the shite in Matsukaze, for example, normally is not) and he is in touch with his enemy via the communion of polar opposites. (In

<u>Yashima</u> the warring forces clash in a mirror-image battle.) Therefore in a warrior play <u>yume</u> and <u>utsutsu</u>, though already distinct, are still patently linked.

Finally I would like to make a few remarks about kyōgen. I have scattered kyōgen among the nō plays without any comment, but I do believe kyōgen to be an integral part of the aesthetic workings of nō. J. S. Bach almost requires the invention of P.D.Q. Bach; and P.D.Q. Bach quickens one's appreciation of the master's genius. I do know that it is a relief and a pleasure to translate a kyōgen after a great nō play, and a pleasure again to turn to nō after a kyōgen. Well-placed irreverance is a wonderful thing. Incidentally, the texts I used for the kyōgen translations are those in the two-volume <u>Kyōgen shū</u> in the <u>Nihon koten bungaku taikei</u> series, edited by Koyama Hiroshi.

TECHNICAL TERMS

The stage   (see diagram on following page)

Bridgeway	hashigakari
Center	mannaka
Curtain	makuguchi
Doer post	shite-bashira
Down front	shōmen-saki
(before) Drums	daishō-mae
First pine	ichi no matsu
Flute post	fue-bashira
Fool's spot	ai-za
Front	shōmen
Main spot	jōza
Mark post	metsuke-bashira
Second pine	ni no matsu
Side	waki shōmen
Sideman's spot	waki-za
Slit door	kirido
Stagehand spot	kōken-za
Third pine	san no matsu

ROLES IN THE PLAYS

DOER:	Shite	FOOL:	Kyōgen
SECOND:	Tsure	CHILD:	Kokata
SIDEMAN:	Waki	CHORUS:	Ji
SIDEMAN'S SECOND:	Waki-zure	STAGEHAND:	Kōken

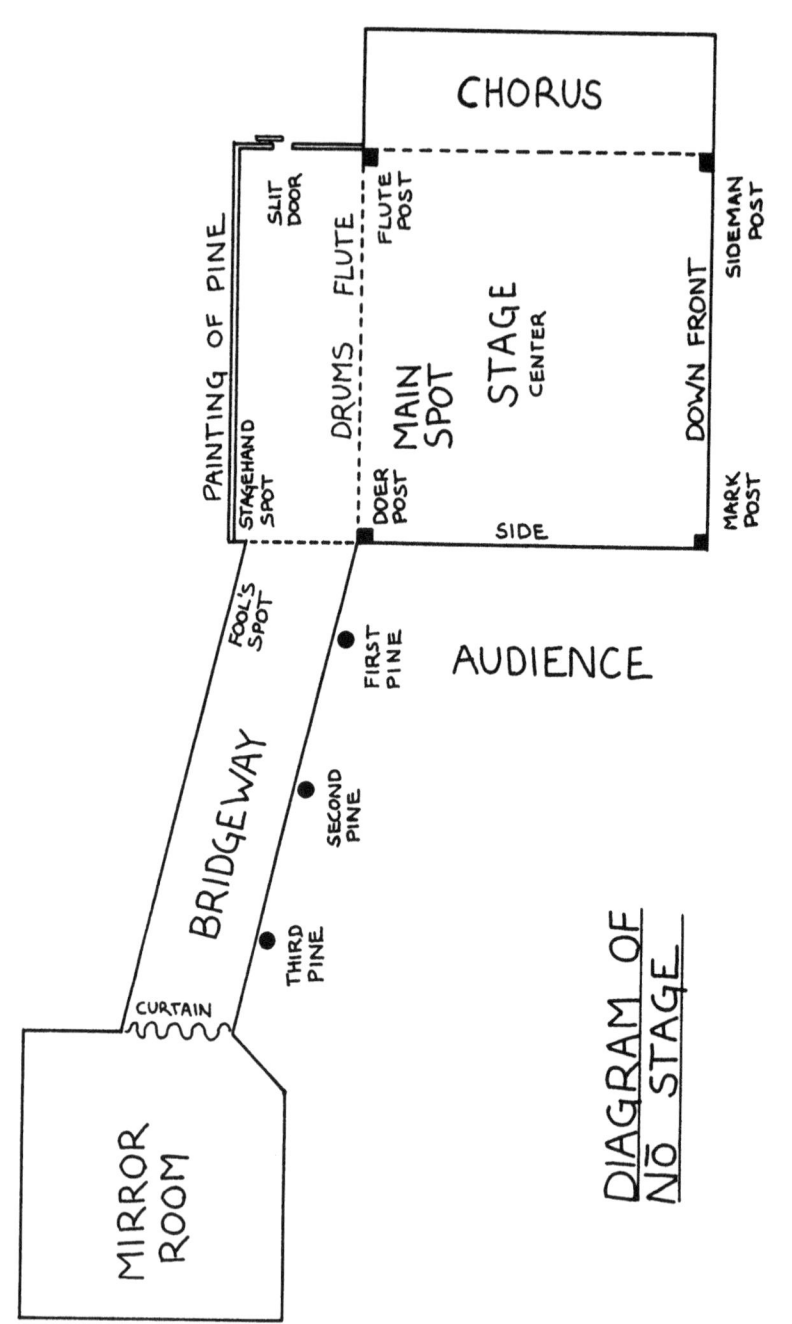

DIAGRAM OF
NŌ STAGE

Movements and Gestures

Clasped fan: kakae ogi. The open fan, held in the right hand, is
  pressed to the left shoulder and the actor gazes a little to
  his right.

Cloud fan: kumo no ogi. The actor joins the open fan, held as
  usual in his right hand, with his left hand, directly in
  front of him; then he spreads these apart and gazes into the
  distance.

(to) Display fan: ogi o kazasu. The open fan is displayed at the
  level of the head.

Excitement: yuken. The open fan is raised and lowered at the level
  of the heart.

Fan high: age-ogi. The open fan is lifted up before the face, then
  lowered toward the right.

Full excitement: ryo-yuken. The gesture of yuken is made with both
  hands.

Full leftright: ozayu. The actor takes several steps while perform-
  ing a leftright.

Leftright: sayu. The actor thrusts his left hand forward and turns
  to the left, then thrusts his right hand forward and turns to
  the right.

(to) Open: hiraku. The actor spreads both arms wide, while taking a
  step and a half backward.

(to) Press toward: tsume-ashi. The actor takes one or two steps
  forward, very intently.

MODES OF DELIVERY OF TEXT

Off: off-beat or non-congruent rhythm, hyōshi awazu

On: on-beat or congruent rhythm, hyōshi au

Ōnori: a particular form of congruent rhythm

S: song, fushi

Sp: speech, kotoba

Str: strong or dynamic mode, tsuyogin. A style of singing

W: weak or melodic mode, yowagin. A style of singing

?   a place where it is unclear if the mode of delivery is

            tsuyogin or yowagin.

These modes of delivery are normally indicated in the left margin under the name of each shōdan, or subdivision of the play. However, when the mode of delivery changes within a shōdan, the change is shown by the presence of the appropriate abbreviation at the head of the passage in which the delivery changes. When, under the name of the shōdan, the mode of delivery is followed by an asterisk, this means that the shōdan contains both speech and song.

THE SUBDIVISIONS OF THE PLAYS

The plays are divided into sections set off by arabic numerals, and further subdivided into shōdan, which are indicated by Japanese names. Both numerals and shōdan names are in the left margin of the text. Where a shōdan has no traditional name, this is shown by an asterisk in the place where the name would normally be given. All shōdan and numbered divisions of the text follow Yokomichi Mario and Omote Akira's Yōkyoku shū, vols. 1 and 2, in Nihon koten bungaku taikei.

THE FEATHER MANTLE
(Hagoromo: a woman play)

This play begins on a perfect spring day: sweeping blue sky,
mild air, pines along the beach, and sunlit sea. The world we know
appeared, they say, when sky and earth split apart; now, though, heaven
and earth seem still conjoined at ease, one lightly-breathing vastness.
As on such a day the earthbound heart rises of itself into free space,
so an angel, too, may, as in The Feather Mantle, descend.

No one knows for certain who wrote The Feather Mantle, or when,
but it makes a fine introduction to the whole nō repertoire. Many of
the marks of a god play can be found in it, and one of these is
thanks given for our Sovereign's reign. This thanks is rendered for
all harmony and delight, to the Lord who shall reign for ever and
ever; whose reign endures, indeed, even through the trials enacted in
the plays that follow. (If his reign did not so endure, then return
to communion and illumination would hardly be possible.) This
Sovereign is not only secular and historical; he is also the focal
point and power·center of the world.

It is the angel's warm, feminine charm that puts The Feather
Mantle in the class of woman plays, for true god plays avoid such
coloring. This very charm, though, makes The Feather Mantle more perfectly representative, for love is the heart of Japanese poetry--
especially if to love between man and woman, one joins love for the
fleeting graces of nature herself.

And who indeed is this charming celestial maiden? She proves to
be the laurel tree that grows in the moon, and the very moon itself,

giver of every gift. Her garment is less a human mantle than sky, mist, and cloud. The flowers in her hair are doubtless actually growing in the green spring hills. She really does have all of nature's fleeting graces, of which the moon is the sign, and might well move one to love.

In nō, mention of the full moon is likely to be coupled, as here, with the Buddhist term True Semblance (shinnyo). True Semblance can loosely be said to mean Reality, but this reality is no absolute to be grasped at and held. True Semblance can be owned or defined no more than the angel's loveliness.

As the moon, the angel invokes her own 'true ground,' the Bodhisattva Seishi. This is because Shinto deities, the natural powers of the world, were widely held to be local manifestations of the universal Buddhas and Bodhisattvas. Such a local manifestation is the projected image, and the name of this mode of understanding is honji suijaku, true ground and projected image. Seishi stands to the right of the Buddha Amida, Lord of Infinite Light, and is Amida's all-illuminating wisdom. Thus the angel, with all her graces, is actually wisdom manifest.

Versions of the story of The Feather Mantle are to be found all over the world. The pattern is that a band of celestial maidens (in ancient Japanese accounts the number is eight) come down to earth to enjoy some particularly wholesome pleasure, such as bathing in a spring or drinking fresh milk. There, a man surprises them. All escape back to heaven but the last one, who is detained by the man and often has to marry him. Much later, though, she does fly home again, and the man, who by some failing has let her escape, can never follow.

What the angel does during her visit to earth is to transmit certain music called the Suruga Dance from East Country Pleasures. East Country Pleasures is <u>Azuma-asobi</u>, a body of songs and dances from the region far to the east of Miyako, the capital. There is a tradition that an angel did indeed give the Suruga Dance to mankind on a beach in the province of Suruga. From the standpoint of nō, however, one might imagine that it is music itself that she teaches, and that the whole repertoire is an unfolding of this music.

ISSEI

(A small pine stands down front. Caught in its branches is a length of cloth that represents the mantle. Sideman and two Sideman's Seconds enter, carrying fishing poles; they stand down front, to one side of the pine. When all three sing together, they are face to face; when Sideman speaks alone, he faces front.)

ISSEI

SIDEMAN AND SIDE SECOND

Swift winds blow   by Mio   down the curving shore small craft row   and fishermen   call o'er the sea lanes!

NANORI

SIDEMAN

I'm a fisherman known on the pine barrens of Mio as Hakuryo.

SASHI

SIDEMAN AND SIDE SECOND

'Boundless leagues of lovely hills, and clouds suddenly rise; one lone tower's bright moon marks first the rain's clearing.' Yes, a time it is   of mild calm! Spring again has touched   pine barrens   wave on lingering wave   the morning mists,   moon loitering in sky meadows   endless   the gaze roves on: a scene to quiet,   to absorb the heart!

SAGEUTA

I'll not forget   how mountain trails   we took to Clearview Cove,   and spied afar   Mio's pine barrens: come now, friends,   there's where we'll go   come now, friends,   there's where we'll go!

AGEUTA

Wind-billowed,   the clouds float high   waves then to you   the clouds float high   waves then to you are they, men,   no fishing done,   will you hurry home?   Wait!   It's spring a while,   and mild blows the morning breeze,   yes, the pines' song everlasting,   waves are silent   in the morning calm and fishermen crowd forth   in teeming craft fishermen crowd forth   in teeming craft!

(Sideman's Seconds sit slightly upstage of
Sideman's spot. Sideman lays down his pole at
stagehand stop, takes fan in hand, and comes out
to main spot.)

*

SIDEMAN   I've just come up to the pine barrens of Mio, and I'm

gazing at the view of the shore, when from the void

blossoms fall, music resounds, and wondrous fragrances

pervade all space. This can hardly be common. And

in fact I see here, hung on this pine tree, a beautiful

mantle. A closer look now: color and scent are

marvelous indeed. This is no ordinary mantle. I'll

take it home with me to show my friends, and to keep

as an heirloom in my house.

(Carrying the mantle in both hands, he
starts toward Sideman's spot. But Doer calls to him
as she comes through curtain, and starts down
bridgeway. She wears the zō-onna mask and an
angel's glittering crown.)

MONDO
DOER   I'm sorry, but that mantle's mine! Why have you

taken it?

(Sideman is now at Sideman's spot.)

SIDEMAN   I just happen to have run across it, so I'm taking it

home with me.

DOER   But it's an angel's feather mantle! It isn't supposed

to be given to a human being! Do please leave it where

it was!

SIDEMAN   As I understand it, then, this is an angel's mantle.

Why, in that case, it's obviously a wonder in these

latter days, and I ought to have it as a treasure for

the whole land! I'm not going to give it back.

DOER   Oh no! Without the feather mantle, flying is over

for me; I'll never be able to return to Heaven!

Please, please give it back!

SIDEMAN   Hakuryō will not heed this gracious plea, but grows stubborn: heartless I've always been, I, a fisherman. The celestial feather mantle he hides from her.

> (He turns front, away from Doer, who is by now at main spot.)

No indeed, says he, and turns to go.

DOER   In her plight now the angel, like a wingless bird,

SIDEMAN   moving to rise, has no mantle;

DOER   on earth, is caught in the nether world.

SIDEMAN   Either way, alas! . . . she laments,

DOER   but as Hakuryō will keep the mantle,

SIDEMAN   helpless,

DOER   hopeless

AGEUTA

CHORUS   tears run, shining jewel headdress, flowers in her hair droop and wilt: the five signs of an angel's fall are here before my very eyes-- oh pitiful!

> (She gazes up to her right into the sky.)

SHIMO-NO-EI

DOER   'To the fields of Heaven backward I gaze, but mists rise, cloudways blur, the path is lost!'

SAGEUTA

CHORUS   My home so dear, the sky, oh when shall I pass yonder move the clouds and enviously I look on!

AGEUTA

The kalavinka's voice I loved the kalavinka's voice I loved to hear, now fades and wild geese cry down the skyways, going home-- and oh, this

longing!   Plovers, gulls,   with waves offshore
come and go   breezes of spring   blowing through
the sky, they too   quicken yearning   blowing
through the sky, they too   quicken yearning!

(She gazes up at sky, and weeps.)

MONDO

SIDEMAN   I can see now you're suffering terribly. I'll give
you back your mantle.

DOER   Oh, I'm so happy! Then do bring it to me!

(She presses toward Sideman.)

SIDEMAN   A moment, though.

(He retreats an equal distance.)

I'll return your mantle if you'll be kind enough to
do right here and now the angel dance I've heard tell
of.

DOER   I'm so happy! Yes, I _will_ get home to Heaven! And
for joy I'll indeed dance, right here and now. You
shall pass my dance on to the downcast folk of your
world. But I can't do anything without my mantle.
Please give it back to me first.

SIDEMAN   Oh no, if I return your mantle you won't dance, you'll
head straight up to Heaven.

DOER   No, suspicion's for the human realm; in Heaven there's
no falsehood.

SIDEMAN   I'm so ashamed! Why then, says he, by all means; and
gives her back the mantle.

MONO-GI-
ASHIRAI

(Side gives mantle to Doer, then goes to
sit at Sideman's spot. Doer withdraws to stagehand
spot, where she puts on the mantle. She then comes
out to main spot.)

KAKEAI

DOER The maiden, in mantle clothed, does Rainbow Skirts
      and Cloak of Wings;

SIDEMAN the celestial feather mantle moves to the winds,

DOER moist with rain the blossom sleeves,

SIDEMAN as music plays

DOER and she dances on!

SHIDAI

CHORUS The Suruga Dance from East Country Pleasures the
        Suruga Dance from East Country Pleasures: surely,
        this is how it began!

KURI

Now, to speak of the long-faring sky: ages past,
in the Twin Gods' time, when they laid out the world
in each one of its ten directions, the sky had
no end, and that it why they dubbed it long-
faring.

SASHI

DOER As for the Palace of the Moon, with glittering
      ax hewn for all eternity:

CHORUS robed in white or black the angel throng made two
        bands, each of thrice five, and all moon long,
        night by night, a celestial maid with task
        assigned carries out her role.

DOER Of these I am one: celestial maiden

CHORUS of the moon laurel tree, I've split in two, to
        visit and myself pass on to your world here the
        Suruga Dance of the East Country!

KUSE

Mists of spring trail on long-faring moon laurel
flowers bloom! Yes, crown of blossoms in full hue
surely means spring! Oh lovely! Though no Heaven,
here too we've sweet grace. Winds of the skies,

blow shut the clouds' passageways! The maiden
lingers, pine barrens' spring hues to see on
Mio Cape, and the moon so Clearview Cove,
snows of Fuji-- which excels? Peerless this
spring dawn, the waves, the pining wind so
mild, the tranquil shore! Sky and earth, why,
what parts them? Zoned with light are Inner Shrine
and Outer, whose gods' offspring rule here still;
the very moon's spotlessly clear our sunrise land,
Japan!

DOER   In this our Sovereign's reign celestial feather
mantles seldom descend:

CHORUS   caressed, the rock yet wears not away, oh happy
news! Songs of the East: with voices join in
sweet concert drone-pipes, flutes, harps and
zitherns swelling out past the Lone Cloud; red
sinks the sun, so mirroring Mount Sumeru; green
in the waves Float Isle Moor gale-swept, where
blossoms fall, yes, whirling snow the white cloud
sleeves are lovely indeed!

                    (Pausing in her dance movements, Doer sits
                at main spot and joins palms in reverence.)

    EI
DOER   Hail to thee, Seishi, oh thou True Ground of the
Moon, daughter of Heaven!

CHORUS   A dance, then, from the East Country Pleasures.
    JO-NO-
    MAI
                    (Doer rises and, between these two passages
                of text, dances a jo-no-mai dance. She goes on
                dancing, however, as text resumes.)

    NORIJI
DOER   Now, the mantle blue that's Heaven's lofty sky,

CHORUS   now, the mantling mist that rises in spring,

DOER   hue and fragrance both delight! The maiden's train

CHORUS   sweeps and sways,   all rustling,   flowers nod in her
hair;   celestial   feather sleeves   billow, coil
and turn,   the dancing sleeves!

HA-NO-
MAI

               (Between these two passages, she dances a
ha-no-mai dance. Again, she continues dancing as
text resumes.)

NORIJI

As on and on   the dances go   as on and on   the
dances go,   she who's named moon   palace lady   high
in the dark sky   this thrice fifth night   becomes
again   face of True Semblance,   the full moon,   and
rains riches: prayers fulfilled,   the realm replete,
the seven treasures   overflowing,   these on our land
bestows;   and so time runs,   the celestial   feather
mantle   wind-borne billows   down the shore;   pine
barrens of Mio,   Float Isle's clouds,   Mount Ashitaka,
yes,   and Fuji's   towering peak   fade out,   mist-
veiled   into high Heaven   she is lost from view.

TAKASAGO
(A god play)

Takasago, by Zeami, is perhaps the best loved of all the god
plays. Its clear tone will endure, all but forgotten, until it is
reaffirmed in a burst of energy at the close of the demon play--here
The Watchmen's Mirror.

Takasago actually means "dune." The area is now an industrial
city on the Inland Sea, but the Takasago Shrine is still there.
Takasago has been famous in poetry since ancient times, and famous
especially for the Takasago Pine. This pine is said to be paired
with the Suminoe Pine, but Sumiyoshi (Suminoe is simply an older form
of the same name) is far to the east, in the neighboring province, and
one wonders how the two pines really can be paired. The answer is
that their perfect attunement frees them from space. Moreover, the
Paired Pines are free of time as well, since one is the distant past
and the other the present.

Nō plays often hint that past and present can be one. In Takasago, the past is called the time of the Man'yōshū, a great anthology
of the earliest Japanese poetry compiled in the eighth century; and
the present is called the time of the Kokinshū, another basic anthology
compiled during the Engi era, in the early tenth century. It is tact-
ful convention that makes the Engi era the present in Takasago; nō
never treats the historical present.

There is much talk of poetry in Takasago, but in a very wide
sense. The principal Japanese word for 'poem' is uta, which more
generally means song. Thus we are told that "each sound of beings

feeling and non-feeling, every last one, is a song." This is why "all living things to the Blessed Isles, they say, draw nigh." For Blessed Isles (a tentative translation of the name _Shikishima_) is an ancient name for the islands of Japan, and here stands for _Shikishima no michi_, the way of the Blessed Isles: this is simply a term for poetry.

The true function of poetry in the Japanese tradition is communication. When all sound is heard as song, that is, as communication of essence, there are no barriers anywhere to understanding. (It is often specifically mentioned in god plays that all barriers, gates, and checkpoints stand open: the roads are free, communications are unimpeded.) When speech is coherent, as light can be coherent, truth is conveyed. The unfailing leaves of speech spoken of in _Takasago_ are an everlasting flow of song that conveys the essence of man, and, in a wider sense, the endless hymn sung by all beings to that other singer, the one source of all being. In this antiphon, both beings and source are at one.

Leaves of speech: one can hardly fail to think of leaves of grass. "Words" is all the term means, and "leaves of speech" (_ha_ is a pine needle as well as a leaf) is an overtranslation. But the metaphor is so often followed up in nō that one must translate it, or mutilate whole passages.

The fool tells the Sideman in _Takasago_ that the Paired Pines hold divine converse through these pine boughs: each needle is, or sings, a word of their song. And since the pine is always green, the song is indeed endless. This endless vigor and life (the pine was said to flower ten times, once every thousand years) are actually seen

in the pine's unchanging hue, and heard in the sound the wind makes
as it blows through a pine tree. <u>Pining Wind</u> is a play about this
sound.

The climax of <u>Takasago</u> is the appearance and dance of the god
pine himself, in the guise of the God of Sumiyoshi. The Sumiyoshi
Shrine, near what is now the city of Osaka, is one of the greatest
shrines in Japan, and the god there is the god of the sea. Perhaps
sea and pine are one because the sea, too, is endlessly and murmurously
alive. At any rate, the young and handsome god might well be nick-
named, like Henri IV of France, Le Vert Galant.

SHIN-NO- SHIDAI SHIDAI on-str	(Sideman and Sideman's Second enter; they stand facing each other down front.)
SIDEMAN AND SIDE SECOND	Now do we first our travel wear now do we first our travel wear day by day it's bound afar we go!

(Sideman faces front)

NANORI off-sp	
SIDEMAN	I here present before you am Tomonari, a priest from the Aso Shrine in Kyushu. As I have not yet seen Miyako, I am starting on up there now; and I mean to take a look at famous spots all along the way.

(They face each other again.)

AGEUTA on-str	
SIDEMAN AND SIDE SECOND	Travel wear, unfolding long Miyako Way unfolding long Miyako Way's cut out for us now waves touch shore and ship lanes lie calm the spring breeze how many days stretch on, ahead, behind, all's vague white clouds trail away,

(Sideman takes a few steps to show travel,
then by the end of the passage returns to his place
and faces front.)

why yes, Harima coast   and Takasago shore   is where
we are   Takasago shore   is where we are.

TSUKI- ZERIFU off-sp	
SIDEMAN	Hurrying along that way, we have come to Takasago shore in the land of Harima. Perhaps someone from nearby will be kind enough to show us the sights.

(Sideman and Sideman's Second retire to
Sideman's spot. Second enters, followed by Doer.
They stop at first and third pines, respectively.
Doer wears the <u>koujijō</u> mask and carries a rake;
Second wears the <u>uba</u> mask and carries a broom.
They face each other.)

SHIN-NO- ISSEI	

ISSEI
off-str

DOER, SECOND   Takasago,   through the High Dune   pine spring
breezes   blow till sundown,   Onoe   the Hilltop
bell   gently tolls.

(Second faces front.)

SECOND   Waves with light mists   veiled from shore

(They face each other.)

DOER, SECOND   sound us the salt tides'   ebb and flow.

(They come onstage. Second stands at
center, Doer at main spot, both facing front.)

SASHI
off-str

DOER   'Who then, who   shall be friend to me?   Takasago's
very pine of old   I never knew';

(They face each other.)

DOER, SECOND   as ages come,   ages gone,   bank snow on what snows
we hoary cranes   roost where lingers   breaking
dawn   by spring nights of rime,   work or rest,
it's pining wind alone   the ear takes in,   while
the heart's   the friend I choose   to open to.

SAGEUTA
on-str

For callers, why,   courting the pines   come shore
winds   and fallen needles cloak   now sleeve by
sleeve,   come, clear litter   from beneath the tree
come, clear litter   from beneath the tree!

AGEUTA
on-str

The place here, Takasago   the place here,   Takasago,
and Hilltop Pine   has grown old,   ripples of age
come wrinkling in,   and all around   under the tree
fallen needles   lie deep-piled,   so enduring   does
life thrive,   and how much longer yet?   The Iki Pine,

>   (Doer moves to center as Second goes to
>   mark post; they face front.)

why, there's another   place of lasting fame
why, there's another   place of lasting fame.

MONDO
off-str*

SIDEMAN   ^{sp}Just as I'm waiting for someone from the village,
an old couple has arrived. Old people, I beg your
pardon, but I have a question for you.

DOER   You're talking to us, sir? What is it?

SIDEMAN   Which of these trees is the Takasago Pine?

DOER   Why, the one this old man is clearing around right
now, that's the Takasago Pine.

SIDEMAN   The Takasago Pine and the Pine of Suminoe are said
to be 'paired,' yet Takasago and Sumiyoshi are a
whole province apart. How is it they're called the
Paired Pines?

DOER   The preface to the <u>Kokinshū</u> says, 'The pines of Takasago and Suminoe are themselves reputed to be paired.'
But this old man is from Sumiyoshi, in yonder land
of Tsu. It's the old lady here who hails from Takasago.

>   (He turns to Second.)

If you know anything about this, do please tell it.

SIDEMAN   ^sAstonishing!   I see, old people,   that you're
together here,   man and wife, yet   far Suminoe
and Takasago,   by shore and mountain   a whole land
apart,   you say are your homes.   How can this be?

SECOND   Strange question!   Though ten thousand leagues   of
hill and stream   divide them,   for lovers' hearts
finely attuned,   the way is never long.

DOER   ^{sp}Just reflect a little.

(Doer and Second face each other.)

DOER, SECOND   ^sThe Takasago,   Suminoe pines,   all insentient,
do still bear   the name of Paired: how much more
we, then,   living humans,   with all the years
we've gladly plied   between here   and Sumiyoshi--
an old couple,   who in the pines'   own company
have until now

        (Doer presses toward Sideman.)

lived on, paired in age.

KAKEAI
off-str*

SIDEMAN   ^sI hear you talk   with greatest pleasure.   Tell
me then: the Paired Pines   you spoke of now,
do people here   draw from them no moral?

DOER   ^{sp}In the old days,   people said they mark   a
happy reign.

SECOND   ^sTakasago means the ancient times of the Man'yōshū;

DOER   ^{sp}and Sumiyoshi, His Majesty of Engi, who dwells in
this present age.

SECOND   ^sPine means unfailing   leaves of speech

DOER   ^{sp}whose vigor endures   now, as then,

DOER, SECOND   ^san image   of praise to this reign.

SIDEMAN   Most willingly   I've heard you out,   and how I
thank you!   Now in me no doubts   spring sunny days

DOER, SECOND   with tempered brightness   light the western sea,

SIDEMAN   and yonder,   Suminoe,

DOER   Takasago here

SIDEMAN   pines gather hue,

        (Doer presses toward Sideman.)

DOER   the spring is mild,

            (Doer faces front, while Second goes to
            stand before Chorus and Sideman sits at Sideman's
            spot. At 'rustles,' Doer advances a little and
            opens; after 'fortune,' he changes mood and goes
            to mark post, then turns left up to main spot;
            at 'of our Lord's,' turns to Sideman, then moves
            to center and sits. Second sits also.)

        AGEUTA
        on-str

CHORUS   the Four Seas calm,   the Realm at peace;   a timely

            breeze   rustles no boughs   in this sovereign reign!

            Well met indeed,   the Paired Pines   show good

            fortune!   No, no praise   is equal to the task,

            for such a reign   brings to us, His subjects,   full

            richness   of our Lord's blessing,   o the precious

            gift!   of our Lord's blessing,   o the precious gift!

        *
        off-sp

SIDEMAN   But do tell me more about the happy meaning of the

            Takasago Pine.

        KURI
        off-str

CHORUS   Now, plants and trees, they say, have no heart, yet

            flower and fruit never miss their time; filled with

            the power of surging spring, the southern boughs it

            is that blossom first.

        SASHI
        off-str

DOER   Yet this pine looks ever the same; the flowers and

            fruit distinguish no time.

CHORUS   The four seasons pass, yet deep its millenial hue

            holds amid the snow; and the pine's very flowers bloom

            ten times, once in ten lives.

DOER   For such news does one pine boughs

CHORUS   bear needle leaves   of speech aglow   with dewdrop

            pearls: these in the heart   seed polished grace,

DOER   till all living things

CHORUS   to the Blessed Isles,   they say, draw nigh.
  KUSE
  on-str

                For indeed,   in Chōnō's words,   'Each sound
                of beings feeling   and non-feeling,   every last
                one,   is a song.'   Plants, trees, soil, sand,
                voice of the wind,   water noises: even there's
                a heart   to harbor all.   Springtime woods
                moving to east wind,   fall insects crying   in
                northern dews: are not both song,   our poetry?
                And the pine   stands over all trees,   in lordly
                guise,   green through a thousand falls,   and
                shows no hue   of new or old: a tree worthy
                of that title,   Marquis,   the First Emperor gave
                it,   so that in China   and this Realm,   all men
                accord it praise.

DOER   'Takasago,   the High Dunes'   Hilltop bell rings;

                        (Doer stands, still holding his rake,
                    and comes down front.)

CHORUS   through to dawn   settles freezing rime,'   yet pine
                boughs'   needles stay   the same deep green.
                Morning and night

                        (He mimes sweeping.)

                I come to clean   beneath the tree,   but fallen
                needles   never fail: for true it is,

                        (He gazes up as though at pine branches.)

                pine needles   do not all fall,   their hue only
                grows and grows   the masaki vine,   sign of an
                enduring reign;   and among all evergreens   the
                Takasago Pine

                        (He turns to Sideman, then moves to center
                    and sits.)

in this late age,   paired still,   signals blessing.

RONGI
on-str

Yes, justly famed,   boughs of this pine,
yes, justly famed,   boughs of this pine   the old
tree's past   do tell, and now,   pray, say your
names!

DOER, SECOND   Then, what need we conceal?   We, the spirits   of
the Paired Pines   of Takasago   and Suminoe,   man
and wife,   stand before you.

CHORUS   Astonishing!   So, the renowned   pines show a
wonder,

DOER, SECOND   and though plants   are without heart,

CHORUS   so wise His rule

DOER, SECOND   that plants and trees, both,

CHORUS   land that this is   of our great Lord,   aspire under
His sovereign reign   to dwell on and

            (Doer turns to Sideman, then points his
        fan toward back of stage.)

on we'll go   to Sumiyoshi now   to wait for you,
cry   they beside

            (He stands, goes to side, and stamps beat
        as though boarding a boat.)

the evening waves   a fishing craft   now board,
and sail   before the wind   far, far away   across
the sea   far, far away   across the sea.

            (Doer and Second exit. Now Sideman addresses
        Sideman's Second, and approximately the following
        dialogue ensues.)

MONDO
off-sp

SIDEMAN   I've a question to ask. Please see if anyone is nearby.

SIDE SECOND   Yes, sir.

> (He goes to main spot.)

Hello! Is anyone around?

> (The Fool, who some time ago slipped
> in to sit at Fool's spot, now stands.)

FOOL   Surely. What can I do for you?

SIDE SECOND   Would you mind coming with me? My master has a question he wishes to ask you.

FOOL   By all means.

> (Sideman's second goes before Sideman.)

SIDE SECOND   Sir, here is someone who will answer your question.

> (He goes to sit before Chorus. Fool sits
> at center.)

SIDEMAN   The Takasago Pine is famous indeed. But could you tell me about its connection with the Pine of Suminoe?

FOOL   Well, I hardly know a thing about it, but I'll tell you what I've heard.

KATARI
off-sp

They say the pines of Takasago and Suminoe stand for the Man'yōshū and the Kokinshū. One story has it that the God of Takasago and the God of Sumiyoshi were man and wife, and that when they called on each other they held divine converse through these pine boughs. That's why the pines are described as Paired. The glory of our own poetry, the vigor of courtship and marriage: for both of these we have the gods' divine power to thank.

> (He goes on to cite various classic texts
> in support of his theme.)

By the way, didn't you meet an old man and an old woman cleaning around the base of the pine here?

SIDEMAN   I did indeed. They spoke of the Paired Pines and of
their fame, then suddenly stepped into a boat and set
sail, they said, for Sumiyoshi.

FOOL   Then no doubt that old couple were the spirits of the
Takasago and Suminoe pines themselves. You really
should go on pilgrimage to Sumiyoshi.

SIDEMAN   But I have no boat.

FOOL   In that case, please do this little craft, newly built
as it is, the honor of being the first to sail it.
It will take you safely to Sumiyoshi. See! A following breeze is blowing!

SIDEMAN   Thank you very much indeed.

FOOL   At your service.

> (Fool retires to Fool's spot. He will slip
> out after the Doer's entrance. Sideman and Sideman's
> Second now face each other down front.)

AGEUTA
on-str

SIDEMAN AND
SIDE SECOND   Takasago!   Our light craft   under all sail   our
light craft   under all sail   slips out   with the
moon   rising, the tide surge swells   waves' salt
foam,   Awaji Isle looms   and drops   far thunders
Naruo   while skimming on   swiftly to Suminoe borne
we have put in   swiftly to Suminoe borne   we have
put in.

> (Sideman and Sideman's Second retire to
> Sideman's spot. Doer, who is now the God of Sumi-
> yoshi, makes a vigorous entrance and stands facing
> front at first pine. He wears the <u>kantan-otoko</u> mask.

DEHA

SASHI
off-str

DOER   'Myself I've watched   these long, long years   on
Sumiyoshi coast,   the lady-pine--   and she,   what
eons has she seen?'   'We're lovers: did my Lord not
know?   Within the Pristine Zone,

            (Doer strikes full excitement pose, then
        stamps several beats.)

down long ages   has the god endured;   music and

mime   now play, night drums   in rhythm beat,

            (He sweeps his gaze over orchestra.)

soothe His heart now,   ye of the Shrine!

            (Now he goes to main spot. At 'rises,' he
        stamps several beats; at 'spring,' points around
        with fan, as though at a still snow-mantled land-
        scape; at 'by the beach,' goes before drums, faces
        front, opens; at 'thousand,' stamps several beats;
        at 'break off,' comes down front, mimes the action
        described, then turns left back up to drums, takes
        left sleeve in right hand, gazes as though at
        petals clinging there.)

KAMI-NO-EI
off-str

CHORUS   Up from the western sea,   wave furrows   of Liveoak

            Plain,

DOER   rises now revealed   the god pine,   and it's spring!

   ISSEI   Lingering snows   thin down Asaka strand
   off-str

CHORUS   and by the beach   where sleek seaweed   is cut and

            garnered,

DOER   but once draw nigh   a pine's stout root,   rub your

            hips there,

CHORUS   and a thousand years'   fresh green   brims from your

            hands;

DOER   break off blossoming plum,   set it in your hair,

CHORUS   and snow of the second moon   sprinkles your cloak.'

   KAMI-MAI   (At main spot now, Doer begins a vigorous
        but elegant dance. As text resumes, he withdraws
        to Doer post.)

   RONGI
   on-str

        O precious vision!   O precious vision!   Clear shines

the moon   at Sumiyoshi   sports the God: with
what new joy   we worship   His own form divine!

> (Doer is now facing front at main spot.
> Below, at 'the pine,' he gazes toward pines on
> bridgeway; then points with fan at his own image
> reflected in the sea down front; at 'For God,'
> goes to mark post, then sweeps left up to center;
> at 'pure,' glances at his own left sleeve, then
> turns right and up to flute; then strikes full
> excitement pose, as though sweeping away demons;
> then moves to center, mimes embracing something,
> stamps beat; at 'Thousand Autumns,' moves down
> front, pointing before him with fan, then rolls
> up the long, hanging length of his sleeves, then
> turns right and up to main spot; at first 'inspires,'
> opens toward front; then faces side and stamps
> final beat.)

DOER

Yes, the varied   dancing maidens' voices ring clear
too,   the pine   of Suminoe   mirrored shows in
Blue Sea Waves   is this, surely!

CHORUS

For God, for Lord,   straight lies the way,   to
Miyako   in springtime go,

DOER

and the dance is   Home to the Palace;

CHORUS

endless fair years they bring,

DOER

the pure, festal robes:

CHORUS

a darting hand   sweeps demons hence,   an arm drawn
in   clasps length of days   and good fortune.   A
Thousand Autumns   brings folk ease;   Ten Thousand
Years   makes life long,   so long the paired
pining wind's   hushed singing sound   inspires
tranquil joy   hushed singing sound   inspires
tranquil joy.

PINEGUM
(Matsuyani)

(Host enters, followed by Tarōkaja. Tarōkaja sits at back of stage, while Host stands at
main spot.)

HOST   I'm a man from the neighborhood. Today I'm holding
my annual pinefest, so I'll just call Tarōkaja and
have him invite everybody. Ahoy! Ahoy! Tarōkaja!
You there?

(He goes to Sideman's spot. Tarōkaja stands.)

TARŌKAJA   YESSIR!

(He comes to main spot.)

HOST   You're here?

TARŌKAJA   Right before you, Sir.

HOST   Good lord, you're fast! There's no panic, you know.
I'm holding a pinefest today, as I do every year.
What do you say?

TARŌKAJA   A wonderful idea, sir, just wonderful.

HOST   Well then, I'm sorry to put you to the trouble, but
do go and get everyone to come.

TARŌKAJA   Very good, sir.

HOST   Tell them, 'Today we're holding our annual pinefest,
so do please all come. And if you'll be kind enough
to sing and dance along with us, we'll be most grateful.'
That's the way to invite them.

TARŌKAJA   Very good, Sir.

HOST   Come right back.

TARŌKAJA   As you wish, sir.

HOST   Away!

TARŌKAJA   YESSIR!

        (Host sits at back of stage. Tarōkaja
stands at main spot.)

My, my, how delightful! He says he's holding the
annual pinefest today, so I'm supposed to go and get
everyone to come. But who am I going to invite? Ah,
Mr. A down the street's the closest. I'll just zip
over there.

        (He starts walking.)

Yep, we do this every year, so I'm sure he won't be
out.

        (After a turn around stage, he stands at
first pine.)

Well, well, here I am. I'll announce myself first.
I say! Beg your pardon!

        (Guest One enters and stands at third pine.)

GUEST ONE	Why, someone's calling out front! Who is it? Who's there?
TARŌKAJA	It's me, sir.
GUEST ONE	Oh, you. You didn't have to call from outside that way! Why didn't you come right on in?
TARŌKAJA	I thought I might do that, but then I thought you might have visitors, so I called.
GUEST ONE	That's very thoughtful of you. Why'd you come, anyway?
TARŌKAJA	I'll tell you right away, sir. Here's my message. 'Today we're holding our annual pinefest, so do please all come. And if you'll be kind enough to sing and dance along with us, we'll be most grateful.'
GUEST ONE	That's very considerate, I'm sure. As we go to your pinefest every year, everyone's already gathered here at my place. We've been waiting because the invitation' a bit late. We'll go right along with you.

TARŌKAJA	You mean I don't have to call on everybody?
GUEST ONE	That's right, you don't have to. You go on ahead.
TARŌKAJA	Well then, sir, I will.
GUEST ONE	Leaving so soon?
TARŌKAJA	So long, sir, so long!
GUEST ONE	Glad you came.
TARŌKAJA	YESSIR!

(He faces front.)

Well, well that's fine, just fine. A big help to
the feet. I'll hurry back.

(Now two scenes are done simultaneously.
Tarōkaja is at main spot, speaking to Host who, when
called, stands and goes to Sideman's spot. Meanwhile,
Guest One is at first pine and talks toward curtain;
when he calls the other Guests, they file onto
Bridgeway.)

TARŌKAJA	Hello! Hello! Are you home, Sir?	GUEST ONE	I say! Are you all there?
HOST	Are you back?	GUEST TWO	We're
TARŌKAJA	I went to Mr. A's	ALL	all here!
	just now, and	GUEST ONE	There was someone
	everyone was there		here just now from
	because they		Mr. B's. Shouldn't
	thought the invi-		we be going?
	tation was late.	GUEST TWO	That's
	They said they'd be	ALL	a wonderful idea!
	right along, sir.	GUEST ONE	Now, now, come along,
HOST	What? They were		come along!
	all there and they	ALL	We're coming! We're
	said they'd be right		coming!
	along?	GUEST ONE	Quickly now, quickly!

TARŌKAJA	That's right, sir. In fact, here they are already.	ALL	By all means!

HOST   I see.

> (Host sits at Sideman's spot, while Tarō-kaja sits before drums. Guests all file onstage and sit lined up along side.)

GUEST ONE   Today

GUEST ONE, ALL   is a happy day!

> (They bow to Host.)

HOST   I'm most grateful to you all for coming.

> (He returns the bow.)

GUEST ONE   And we're most grateful to you for having, as always, been kind enough to invite us.

HOST   Well, now, gentlemen, in my opinion, pinegum is extremely felicitous. And so this year I've been thinking of celebrating pinegum. What do you say?

GUEST ONE   An absolutely

GUEST ONE, ALL   wonderful idea.

HOST   In that case, everyone please come right this way.

GUEST ONE, ALL   By all means!

> (All stand lined up behind Host along where the nō Chorus sits.)

HOST   Then on with the celebration!

GUEST ONE, ALL   Yes indeed!

HOST, GUEST ONE, ALL   Pinegum gum o, pinegum gum o, pinegum gum o, my pinegum o!

> (They beat time on their left hand with fan they hold in their right. The song goes on for some time, with the help of drums. Then

                Pinegum enters, mingling his voice with the voices
                of the singers, and stops at first pine. He wears
                the <u>usobuki</u> mask.)

PINEGUM	Gum o, gum o, gum o, pinegum gum o!
HOST	What in the world? Some funny creature's shown up.
GUEST ONE	You're right, something's shown up.
HOST	I'll go and try talking to it.
GUEST ONE	That's
GUEST ONE, ALL	an excellent idea!

                    (Host goes to the stage end of bridgeway.)

HOST	Ahoy! Ahoy! Who are you over there?
PINEGUM	I'm the pinegum spirit. On happy occasions, they say, mighty hermits themselves come down from the mountains, and sages pop up everywhere. The way you've been celebrating me, you've made me so cheerful that I, the pinegum spirit in person, am showing myself to you here.
HOST	That's a happy event indeed. Just wait right there.
PINEGUM	By all means.

                    (Host goes to center and faces Guests.)

HOST	I say! I say! I asked him, and he says he's the pinegum spirit.
GUEST ONE	He really does.
HOST	So let's ask him about all the happy features of the pine.
GUEST ONE	An excellent idea.

                    (Host goes to end of bridgeway again.)

HOST   I say, sir, I say! Do please tell us all about the happy features of the pine!

PINEGUM   By all means. The pine's happy features are that once it's an inch tall, its hue is eternal, and that it lives on a thousand, ten thousand years. Happy it is!

HOST   Extremely happy!

                  (He goes to center and faces Guests.)

             I say! I say! All of you!

GUEST ONE   What?

HOST   What do you think? A happy spirit he is! And what's more, as we've all been practicing archery lately, I think we might cook that pinegum into bowstring resin. What do you say?

GUEST ONE   An absolutely

GUEST ONE,   wonderful idea.
ALL

HOST   In that case, I'll make the proposition

                  (He goes once more to end of bridgeway.)

             Ahem, ahem.

PINEGUM   What is it?

HOST   Everyone says this is a wonderfully happy event. And fortunately, since we've all been practicing archery, we feel we'd like to cook you into bowstring resin. Won't you please let us do that?

PINEGUM   I'm terribly sorry; I'd love to let you, since you're celebrating pinegum so well, but I'm sure you'd do it all wrong. If it's to be done, I'd rather do it for you. What do you say?

HOST   That's an excellent idea. Do please go right ahead.

PINEGUM   By all means.

                          (Host goes back to his place with Guests
                 and all sit. Meanwhile, Chorus files in through
                 slit door and sits at back of stage. Pinegum
                 now comes onstage.)

                 Come, come, now to cook up bowstring resin, says he

                          (He dances a lively <u>kakeri</u> dance, to
                 accompaniment of flute and drums.)

                 come, come, now to cook up bowstring resin, says he.

                          (He goes on dancing as the Chorus sings.)

CHORUS   Stretch wide the resin skin, put the pinegum in; make

                 it thick and sticky, as resin should be, says he,

                 and cooked perfectly, he's going his way. The bow-

                 string to homes brings peace, the bowstring to homes

                 brings peace: we'll draw it now on and on with good

                 pinegum!

                          (The song over, Pinegum exits, followed by
                 Host and Guests. Chorus leaves again by slit door.)

YASHIMA
(A Warrior Play)

It is still spring, with all spring's mists and mild airs, but soon a strong wind rises and we are shown the realm of war: the realm of the Ashuras. This is a realm just below the human, inhabited by beings who are in constant combat. The soul of a warrior who has died in battle is especially likely to go there. Ashuras is one of the Six Ways, the six realms of transmigration: Hell, Beasts, Starving Ghosts, Ashuras, Humans, and Heavenly Beings.

In the second half of the twelfth century, two great warrior clans fought for supremacy in Japan. Of the two, the Taira first had a short time of glory, but they were soon destroyed by the Minamoto. The founder of Minamoto power was Minamoto no Yoritomo (1147-1199), and it was Yoshitsune (1159-1189), one of his younger brothers, who won the three crucial battles against the Taira: Ichi-no-tani, Yashima, and Dan-no-ura.

Yoshitsune is without a doubt Japan's greatest romantic hero. His brilliant exploits coupled with his tragic end--he had to flee his brother's wrath all over Japan, to die at last under attack in the north--have given him an immortal appeal, and there are endless stories and plays about him. The origin of Yoshitsune's woes is the villainous Kajiwara Kagetoki, a rival general who denounced Yoshitsune to Yoritomo.

The battle of Yashima took place in 1185. Having been routed on the mainland coast at Ichi-no-tani, not far from the Suma of Pining Wind, the Taira took to their ships and fled to the northeast coast of

Shikoku. When Yoshitsune caught up with them, he had less than a hundred men, but his daring, and the enemy's blunders, allowed him to put the Taira to flight once more. Then the full Minamoto fleet appeared. At Dan-no-ura, off the southern tip of Honshu, the Taira were annihilated at last.

The tale is told at length in the epic chronicle of those times, the Heike monogatari, but whoever wrote Yashima pruned and re-arranged the story with great skill. Zeami knew Yashima, but it cannot be proven to be by him. There is something in its ease, spaciousness, and sympathetic tone that recalls Komachi at Gateway Temple, another great play whose author is unknown. It also has much in common with Pining Wind.

In Yashima, Yoshitsune is a phantom, first partially, then fully, revealed. Such a phantom is a being whose body has died but who is caught on a low plane of existence where beings, though disincarnate, are not wise. On the contrary, most phantoms in nō cling to the memory of their incarnate life. Often their clinging brings them back to Jambudvīpa, to the scene of their greatest love, their strongest hate, their most hellish anxiety, their most intense misery.

Jambudvīpa (a Sanskrit word which becomes Embu in Japanese) is, in Buddhist cosmology, the continent on which men live. It is south of Mount Sumeru, the central mountain of the universe. The sea of birth-and-death of which Yashima often speaks is life in Jambudvīpa: life as it is lived by beings there, who cling to things, and especially to life itself, and avert their eyes from death. This clinging imprisons them, even if it is clinging to honor itself; or even if, as in The Block, the clinging could hardly be more forgivable.

Yoshitsune's supreme moment in Yashima is his recovery of the
bow he had dropped into the sea. The Heike monogatari says that if
his bow had been truly a mighty one, like that of his father, he would
glady have let the enemy take it. But his bow was not mighty, and he
feared that the Taira would jeer at him when they got it. The
glorious Yoshitsune, of so magnanimous a spirit, seems actually to
have been a rather small man.

SHIDAI   (Sideman and Sideman's Second enter; they
                         stand facing each other down front.)

SHIDAI
on-w
SIDEMAN AND   Moon's southward   to the ocean plains   moon's
SIDE SECOND   southward   to the ocean plains   away we're bound
                for Yashima shore!

                         (Sideman faces front.)

NANORI
off-sp
SIDEMAN   I'm a brother from near Miyako. Since I've never seen
                Shikoku, I've made up my mind to tramp on to the lands
                of the West.

                         (He faces Sideman's Second.)

AGEUTA
on-w
SIDEMAN AND   Mists of spring   lightly rising waves   seaborne sail
SIDE SECOND   we   as westering sun   sets clouds ablaze   the trail
                now   on yonder sky   intent we fare

                         (Sideman takes a few steps to show travel.
                      By the end of the passage he is back in place and
                      faces front.)

                down ship lanes   endless once,   till Yashima shore
                we've reached at last   till Yashima shore   we've
                reached at last.

TSUKI-
ZERIFU
off-sp
SIDEMAN   Hurrying along that way, we've come to Yashima shore,
                as it's called, in the land of Sanuki. The sun's
                almost down, so let's go up to this salt shed and see
                the night through here.

                         (Sideman and Sideman's Second retire to
                      Sideman's spot. Doer, wearing the asakura-jō
ISSEI   mask, then enters, preceded by Second, who does
                not wear a mask. Second stops at first pine,
                Doer at third. Both carry fishing poles.)

SASHI
off-str

DOER What beauty! Now moon's on the sea, billows are like night fires.

SECOND 'An old fisherman, with dark, puts in to the west bank;

DOER at dawn he draws Shō river water, and lights bamboo of So':

(They face each other.)

DOER, SECOND a scene now come alive. The rush fire's glow hints at things half seen, and terrible!

ISSEI
off-str Moon's high tide ocean waves

(Second faces front.)

SECOND in mist the skiff glides on

(They face each other.)

DOER, SECOND till seafolk call: the village is at hand.

(Second moves to center, Doer to main spot. They face front.)

SASHI
off-str

DOER One leaf, a skiff runs ten thousand leagues, for will only the wind in its one sail.

SECOND In twilight sky cloud billows

(They face each other.)

DOER, SECOND vanish where the moon goes, through the mist pine woods stand mirrored in deep green, sea and shore fuse; on to Tsukushi of mystic fires must this same sea run!

SAGEUTA
on-str At Yashima, here along the shore, seafolk's dwellings everywhere

AGEUTA
on-str

> fishing keeps us   out over the waves   fishing keeps
> us   out over the waves   mist spreads a veil   till,
> ocean-bound,   seafolk's craft   loom vague   in
> lingering light.   The shore wind too   blows mild,
> as to the heart   spring comes beckoning   as to the
> heart   spring comes beckoning.

TSUKI-
ZERIFU
off-sp

DOER   Let's go directly to rest in the salt shed.

> (Doer sits on a stool before drums, while
> Second sits normally, slightly behind Doer, and
> to his right. Sideman stands, and faces front.)

MONDO
off-str*

SIDEMAN   <u>sp</u>The owner of the salt shed is back. I'll go over
there and get us shelter for the night.

(He turns to Doer and Second.)

Excuse me, there in the salt shed! I beg your pardon!

(Second stands and comes forward.)

SECOND   Who is it?

SIDEMAN   We're monks who are taking a look at all lands.
Please let us have shelter for the night.

SECOND   Wait just a moment. I'll have to ask the owner.

(He turns to Doer and goes down on one knee.)

Excuse me, but some travelers are here, and they say
they'd like shelter for the night.

DOER   What's that? Some travelers are here, and they say
they'd like shelter for the night?

SECOND   Yes.

DOER   That's a simple enough request, certainly, but the
              salt shed in here isn't fit to be seen. Please tell
              them we really can't have them stay.

                        (Second stands, turns to Sideman.)

SECOND   I beg your pardon, but I asked about shelter for you.
              The owner says that as the salt shed in here isn't
              fit to be seen, we really can't have you stay.

SIDEMAN   No, no, we won't mind at all that it's not fit to be
              seen. We're from Miyako, you see. This is our first
              visit to this shore, and we've been caught by sundown.
              Do please repeat my request for a night's shelter.

SECOND   Very well, I will.

                            (He turns to Doer and goes down on one
                          knee as before.)

              I passed on what you said just now. The travelers
              are from Miyako, and as the sun's already down, they
              insist on repeating their request for a night's
              shelter.

DOER   What? You say the travelers are from Miyako?

SECOND   Yes indeed.

DOER   Why, that's dreadful!

                        (He addresses Sideman.)

              I certainly will give you shelter.

SECOND   ⁻ˢThis home of ours   is no more   than a reed-roofed
              hut;

DOER   ⁻ˢᵖfor you, then,   let it be   a simple camping place.

SECOND   ⁻ˢStill, tonight,   'no full beams shine;

                        (Doer looks up at sky.)

DOER   fogged, translucent sky   this spring

                        (Doer and Second face each other.)

DOER, SECOND   night of veiled moon   allows no peer,'   nor quilt
have we,   the seafolk

> (Doer stands, moves away from stool, and
> sits facing Sideman.)

UTA
on-str

CHORUS   hard up by Yashima   the high pines stand,   moss
spreads below: a dismal couch!

> (Sideman takes a couple of steps forward
> and sits. He is in the salt shed, and Sideman's
> Second is felt to have entered as well. Doer
> faces front, while Second goes to sit before
> Chorus.)

AGEUTA
on-w

Come, for comfort, see   down Mure shore   come, for
comfort, see   down Mure shore,   the flocking cranes!
Might they not well return   to their cloud dwelling?

> (Doer turns to Sideman and, deeply moved,
> looks down.)

Ah, travelers,   when I hear your home   is Miyako,
I miss it so!   Yes, we too, once . . .   says he,
but soon, for tears,

> (Doer hides tears.)

can say no more   but soon, for tears,   can say no
more.

> (He turns front again.)

*
off-sp

SIDEMAN   I'm sorry, this subject is hardly one a monk ought to
bring up, but I understand this is the battlefield
where Minamoto and Taira fought. Won't you please
while away the night by telling us the story of that
time?

DOER   Yes, I am surprised at your request. But you're my
guests, and instead of the meal I can't offer you, I

will indeed tell you the tale.

(Doer sits at center on the stool.)

KATARI
off-str*

^{sp}Well now, it was the third moon, the eighteenth
day, in the first year of Genryaku. The Taira fleet
was riding about a hundred yards offshore, when the
Minamoto burst onto the beach. Their field marshal,
in red brocade, and clad in resplendent armor tied
with purple cords,

(Doer draws very erect and glares ahead.)

rose in his stirrups, and boldly proclaimed his name:
His Cloistered Majesty's Envoy, Field Marshal of the
Minamoto Forces, Censor of the Fifth Rank, Minamoto
no Yoshitsune!

(Doer relaxes slightly.)

^{s}Ah, I remember his mighty presence, his true general's
air, as if it were now!

KAKEAI
off-str*

SECOND

^{s}Then among the Taira, all quarreling ceased. ^{sp}One
ship of theirs put in to shore, and, disembarked upon
the wave-washed strand, the warriors defied their
land-based foe.

DOER

So from the Minamoto, in quick response, there galloped
forth fifty mounted men; and among them, shouting out
his name, sped Mionoya no Shirō, at the point of the
charge.

SECOND

^{s}From the Taira side, Akushichibyōe Kagekiyo flung
out his name, ^{sp} and closed with Mionoya.

DOER

In their struggle, Mionoya's sword was shattered. He
fell back somewhat, to the water's edge,

SECOND ^{s}where Kagekiyo fell upon him. Mionoya's

                         (Doer draws very erect, as before.)

DOER ^{sp}neckpiece he seized,

SECOND ^{s}and pulled him back. Then Mionoya

DOER ^{sp}tugged forward to get away:

                         (Doer points forward with fan held, as
                         usual, in right hand; then lays his left hand
                         on his right.)

SECOND ^{s}so, tug and heave

DOER   they pulled, with brute force,

                         (Below, at 'tore,' Doer suddenly pulls
                         back his fan; at 'one side,' glances left and
                         right; at 'When,' gazes intently ahead; at 'rode,'
                         stands and advances slightly to his left; at
                         'Satō,' points toward mark post with fan; at
                         'crashed,' stamps a beat; at 'page,' gazes ahead
                         into distance; at 'both sides,' advances a little;
                         at 'fleet,' looks toward front, then toward cur-
                         tain; at 'battle tide,' turns right and up to
                         main spot; at 'died away,' sweeps his gaze around,
                         low, toward side; then, intently listening, moves
                         to center and sits. Meanwhile, toward the be-
                         ginning of this passage, Sideman retires back to
                         Sideman's spot.)

    UTA
    on-str

CHORUS   till neckpiece tore from helmet and, one to one side

and one to the other, they hurtled headlong. When,

struck by the sight, Yoshitsune rode down to the water,

Satō Tsuginobu intercepted an arrow from the bow of the

Lord of Noto, and crashed from his horse; while aboard

ship, the Lord's page was cut down. Perhaps because

both sides mourned, the fleet withdrew to sea and the

army to camp; the battle tide ebbed till war cries had

died away. Alone remained to be heard the bleak sound

of breakers, and the pining wind.

RONGI
on-w

> How very strange,   you fishermen's   how very
> strange,   you fishermen's   account, far too exact.
> Now, if you please,   tell your names!

DOER, SECOND   Our names--why need you   no more waves this dark
even   tide's withdrawing now;   were this, of course,
the log house   of Asakura,

> (Both turn a moment to Sideman.)

we might say,   as we pass by,   our names . . .

CHORUS   The more you say,   the more I long   to know your
names,   old men

DOER, SECOND   we are,   yes, many signs   tell of our past,   who
we are

CHORUS   and when

DOER, SECOND   the spring night

CHORUS   tide is going out   till soon, at dawn,   comes the
hour   of the Ashuras:

> (They fix Sideman intently with their
> gaze.)

it's then we'll tell our names.

> (They face front again. Doer stands and
> goes to main spot. At 'your dream,' he stares
> again at Sideman and opens, then turns toward
> bridgeway.)

But whether we tell you or no,   in this sad life's
field marshal   your dream,   wake not, nor let it
fade   your dream,   wake not, nor let it fade!

> (Doer exits, followed by Second. Now Fool,
> who for some time past has been sitting at Fool's
> spot, comes out to main spot.)

MONDO
off-sp

FOOL   I'm a fellow who lives on Yashima shore. Right now, I believe I'll have a look around the salt shed here. Why, there are people in there! What do you mean by invading my salt shed without the slightest permission?

SIDEMAN   We're pilgrim monks. We got caught here by sundown, you see, and we had to have shelter for the night.

FOOL   Well then, I suppose it's all right.

SIDEMAN   But perhaps you could tell us something about the battle that took place here between the Taira and the Minamoto forces.

FOOL   I don't know much about things like that, but I'll tell you what I've heard.

KATARI
off-sp

                (He sits at center, and tells the story
        of the encounter between Kagekiyo and Mionoya.)

. . . Yes, it was a real tug-of-war. Finally, the neckpiece tore off, and they both went flying in opposite directions. Mionoya landed, splat, flat on his face, and mashed up his nose. Kagekiyo whomped down on his back, and got a big lump on the back of his head.

SIDEMAN   Thank you very much for your story. An old man who was here a while ago told us the very same one.

FOOL   Did he! Then he must have been Field Marshal Yoshitsune's phantom. You really should stay on, and comfort his shade.

SIDEMAN   Why then, we will.

FOOL   And if you need anything, just call!

                (Fool returns to Fool's spot. He will slip
        out after the Doer's entrance.)

*
off-w*

SIDEMAN   ^{sp}Astonishing! When I asked the old man   for his
             name, he answered,   in this sad life's   field
             marshal   your dream vision,   ^swait, let it not fade,

AGEUTA
on-w

SIDEMAN AND with voice through the hours   whispering   shore winds
SIDE SECOND pine   roots it is   we'll have for pillow,   let the
             heart   unfold   a mat of moss   and once more   await
             the promised dream   and once more   await the prom-
             ised dream.

ISSEI

                        (Doer enters, now wearing the heida mask,
                        and in full battle-dress. He faces front from
                        main spot.)

SASHI
off-str

DOER   'The fallen flower returns not to the bough; the
             shattered mirror never again will shine. Nonetheless,
             in my rage   of wrongful clinging,   I rejoined the
             world   of demon souls

                        (He turns to Sideman.)

             and soon enough,   in agony,

                        (He stamps several beats, then opens.)

             to the Ashuras'   battlefield   swept on, a wave
             hardly shallow   this karma I bear!

KAKEAI
off-str*

SIDEMAN   ^sDawn's close now, I know,   and from where I lie
             watchful, I see   one in full armor clad: could you
             be   the Field Marshal of the Minamoto?

DOER   ^{sp}I am Yoshitsune's phantom. Wrongful clinging, drawn
             on by rage, has me roaming yet the waves of the
             western ocean.

                        (He gazes at Sideman.)

<u>S</u> Engulfed am I   in the sea   of birth-and-death.

SIDEMAN   Oh foolish man!   It's your heart   that makes you

               see   the ocean   of being born,   of dying: True

               Semblance, now,   the moon's

DOER   high this spring night   and spotless too   the

               heart clears,   and the sky.

SIDEMAN   The old days as now   are brought back to mind,

DOER   the way we fought   between ship and shore,

SIDEMAN   yes, on this spot,

                    (Doer presses toward Sideman.)

DOER   there's no forgetting

                        (He opens; at 'bow,' stamps beat; at
                    'archers,' advances slightly; at 'straight,'
                    stamps several beats; at 'birth-and-death,'
                    points at Sideman with left hand, flips left
                    sleeve over, continues staring; at 'here and
                    there,' turns left up to main spot, where he
                    faces Sideman.)

AGEUTA
on-str

CHORUS   the warriors   driving in to Yashima,   bow in hand

               driving in to Yashima,   bow in hand,   and archers

               true,   nor here ever   straight they followed   their

               calling,   yet wayward went,   by birth-and-death's

               seas and mountains   imprisoned,   for back again

               to Yashima   surely I come,   in bitter anger!

               Here and there still   clinging lingers   this deep

               night on the sea   in dream my tale   I'll tell for

               you   in dream my tale   I'll tell for you.

                        (Doer moves to center, where he sits on a
                    stool.)

KURI
off-str

               I can't forget,   though since I left   my old home,

               Jambudvīpa,   long, long years   have passed   by

dreamways   I this night   have come to you
to show you   the Ashura realm.

SASHI
off-str

DOER   Oh, how it comes back,   that spring of old: the
moon, as now,   brilliantly clear

CHORUS   and that shore this same shore!   Minamoto and Taira
stood,   battle-ready,   bows drawn, fleet in formation,
and horses abreast.   Then, at each stride   plunging
and splashing waves   up to our bridles   we pressed
our assault.

KAKEAI
off-str*

DOER ^{sp}That instant, for no good reason, Yoshitsune
dropped his bow.

(Doer draws erect, gazes ahead.)

CHORUS ^{s} The tide just then was on the ebb, and the bow
drifted out to sea.

DOER ^{sp} I'll not let the enemy have my bow! he cried, and
swam his horse through the waves, very near the foe's
ships.

CHORUS ^{s} The enemy saw him, sailed close, and readied a
grappling hook: the peril was great,

DOER ^{sp} but he blocked the hook, broke it, got back his
bow,

(He relaxes a little.)

and made his way up on the beach.

SASHI
off-str

CHORUS   Then Kanefusa made bold to protest: You should never
have done that, sir. Kagetoki meant just this, at
Watanabe. Would you trade your own life for a bow,
even one worth a thousand pieces in gold? So with

tears in his eyes he spoke. Yoshitsune listened, and
answered: By no means, it's not that I clung to the
bow.

KUSE
on-str

Yoshitsune now   among the warriors   of Taira and
Minamoto   takes up the bow   for no selfish motive.
My full fame, however,   is not yet half won;
and if with his bow   now in the foe's hands,
Yoshitsune were jeered at,   called 'little weakling,'
the hurt would be great.   Killed I might have been,
indeed,   but could do nothing else.   Realize that
this,   for Yoshitsune,   was make or break.   As I
live,   I'll not let the enemy have it,   thought I,
for he who takes up the bow,   does he not leave his
name   to all who come after?   So he pleaded,   and
Kanefusa,   indeed, each man present,   shed tears of
heartfelt assent.

DOER   'The wise man is unconfused;

                        (He stands and comes down front.)

CHORUS   the brave knows no fear';   with valiant heart   he
                holds to his good bow

                        (He stamps several beats.)

                lest the foe rob him of it,   and this he does   for
                honor's sake;   but to life holds not,   which giving
                up   he leaves to history   a glorious name,

                        (He opens toward front.)

                worthy of record.

                        (He stamps several beats.)

EI
off-str

DOER   Again, war howls   of the Ashura realm,

CHORUS   and archers' yells,   shake the earth.

KAKERI

>(He now goes to mark post, sweeps left up
to drums, stamps many beats, comes down front,
then turns right up to main spot. During this
interlude, the rhythm changes several times, thus
expressing agitation. As text resumes, Doer stands
at main spot, looking toward side.)

*
off-str

DOER <u>sp</u> Who today is my Ashura foe? What? Noritsune,

Lord of Noto, you say?

>(He strikes excitement pose.)

Aha! A great one! And well-tried, I know!

>(Now he sweeps his pointing fan around to
his right, gazing with it. At first 'seafight,'
he stamps several beats, then comes down front with
a full leftright; at 'mountains,' turns right up to
main spot; at 'from ships,' looks front; at
'ashore,' looks toward curtain, takes fan in left
hand, and draws sword; at 'salt tide,' stamps,
looks down, stamps again; at 'water,' turns left
up to main spot, holds fan like a shield, and advances toward side; at 'clash,' cuts and thrusts
with sword, then retreats toward drums; at 'lift,'
goes down on one knee, pivots to face front, drops
sword; at 'spring night,' strikes cloud fan pose;
at 'foemen,' stands, goes to mark post and thence
to Sideman's spot; at first 'wind,' goes via mark
post to main spot, pointing before him with fan;
at second 'high pines,' opens toward front, then
faces side and stamps final beat.)

<u>s</u> Yes, I do remember   Dan no Ura,

CHU-
NORIJI
on-str

CHORUS   that mighty sea fight   whence I now come   that

mighty sea fight   whence I now come   back to

Jambudvīpa,   to birth-and-death.   Sea and mountains

at one, quake: from ships, war howls;

DOER   ashore, shields like waves;

CHORUS   glinting, moon-struck,

DOER   the fire of swords;

CHORUS   salt tide mirrored,

DOER   helmet stars:

CHORUS   water and sky, sky running on in cloud billows,
thundering clash, counterclash, the fleet's
struggle, thrust and retreat, lift and plunge,
rage on till spring night waves yield up dawn.
Foemen the eye saw were flocking gulls, what the
ear heard as war howls, wind down the shore
through high pines rushing wind down the shore
through high pines raging, a morning gale, no more.

THUNDERBOLT
(Kaminari)

(To music, Doctor enters and stands at
main spot facing back of stage.)

DOCTOR No medicines has he,   the country quack   no medicines has he,   the country quack   knows yellowbark
cures anything.

(He faces front.)

I'm a doctor who lives right in Miyako. These days
there are so many good doctors in town, with titles
like Neurosurgeon, Pediatrician, etc., that country
quacks like me can't get anyone even to let us take a
pulse. It's very hard. But from what I hear, in the
East they're really scraping the bottom of the barrel
for doctors. That's why I'm headed down to the East
right now, to get me a job. Well, I'll just ease on
along.

(He starts walking around the stage.)

Miyako of the countless blossoms has always been home
to me, you know, and I really don't want to give it
up now and head on down to the East. But I've no
choice, I've got to make a living. Anyway, if I
strike it lucky, I'm sure I'll go back to Miyako.

(He stops at center.)

My, after all that way, I've come out on a vast plain.
I've no idea what it's called. What's this? Suddenly
the sky's all clouded over and it's thundering. I'd
better not stay too long around a place like this;
I'm going to hurry on closer to a village.

(He walks toward bridgeway.)

I do hope it doesn't thunder too loud before I get to
a village; I don't like the atmosphere around here.

(Thunderbolt enters, wearing the <u>buaku</u> mask. He has a drumstick in each hand and a double-ended drum slung at his waist. He beats the drum and bawls:)

THUNDERBOLT   Wham, wham, wham, bang, bang!

(Doctor runs into him on bridgeway and yells a spell against lightning. Mulberries were thought to be lightning-proof.)

DOCTOR   Ow, mulberry, mulberry!

(In the process of escaping, Doctor runs once around stage and ends up cowering at Sideman's spot. Thunderbolt pursues him, but suddenly collapses at center.)

THUNDERBOLT   Wham, wham, wham, bang, bang, bang, bang, kaboom! Ouch! Ouch! Ow! Ow! Owowow!

(He gets up, then sits.)

I was having a wonderful time today, crackling and banging around the sky, when all of a sudden I stepped through a gap in the clouds, fell right here, and whacked my butt a terrible blow. I don't even see a tree to help myself back up by.

(He looks toward Sideman's spot.)

Say, there's something there! Hey! Hey! You over there!

DOCTOR   YESSIR!

THUNDERBOLT   What are you?

DOCTOR   I'm a doctor, sir.

THUNDERBOLT   You're what? A dock burr?

DOCTOR   Yes indeed.

THUNDERBOLT   Dock burrs can't talk!

DOCTOR   No, I said doctor. My trade is to cure people's ailments.

THUNDERBOLT   What? You're a doctor and you cure people's ailments?

DOCTOR   That's correct.

THUNDERBOLT   But I'd have you know I'm a thunderbolt!

DOCTOR   YESSIR!

THUNDERBOLT   I was having a wonderful time today, crackling and
               banging around the sky, when all of a sudden I stepped
               through a gap in the clouds, fell right here, and
               whacked my butt a terrible blow. If you're a real
               doctor, cure my butt for me!

DOCTOR   Willingly, sir, but it's the ailments of humans I cure.
               I've never worked on a distinguished thunderbolt be-
               fore. Please allow me to forgo the privilege.

THUNDERBOLT   Why, you pipsqueak, are humans different from thunder-
               bolts? If you're going to talk like that and won't
               cure me, I'll tear you apart.

DOCTOR   Oh no, sir! I'll cure you, I'll cure you!

THUNDERBOLT   Then hop to it.

DOCTOR   First, sir, I'll check your pulse.

THUNDERBOLT   Pulse?

DOCTOR   A human being's pulse is checked at either wrist.
               But for a distinguished thunderbolt, we make what's
               known as a head pulse check.

THUNDERBOLT   My, my! You really know your business, don't you!

DOCTOR   YESSIR!

THUNDERBOLT   Then make it fast!

DOCTOR   By all means, sir!

                      (Doctor goes behind Thunderbolt and twists
                  his head enthusiastically round and round.)

THUNDERBOLT   What are you doing?

(Doctor goes back to Sideman's spot.)

DOCTOR I checked it, sir.

THUNDERBOLT Well?

DOCTOR My diagnosis is that the distinguished thunderbolt is afflicted with dysphoria.

THUNDERBOLT Whew, you're really fantastic! I'm afflicted with dysphoria, huh?

DOCTOR Precisely, sir. If we were at my office now, I could give you medicine for it. But out here in the middle of nowhere, I'll treat you instead with a needle.

THUNDERBOLT A needle?

DOCTOR Just a moment, sir, I'll show you.

    (He unhitches the big needle and mallet he has hanging from his belt, and shows them to Thunderbolt.)

Here it is, sir.

THUNDERBOLT What do you do with that?

DOCTOR I insert it, sir, into the seat of the pain.

THUNDERBOLT You mean you're going to stick a thing like that into me?

DOCTOR Sir, I insert it even into humans. For a distinguished thunderbolt to refuse the operation would mark him as a coward.

THUNDERBOLT Impossible! You stick that thing into humans?

DOCTOR Yes indeed, sir.

THUNDERBOLT Well, if people can take it, a thunderbolt's going to have to, too. Go ahead, stick it in.

DOCTOR I will, sir. But first, sir, please lie down.

THUNDERBOLT Fine. Puff, grunt, groan.

                        (He lies down facing side. Doctor comes
                    up to him.)

DOCTOR   Is it about here, sir?

THUNDERBOLT   Right, just about there.

DOCTOR   Then I'll knock it in, sir.

THUNDERBOLT   Make it fast!

DOCTOR   Certainly, sir.

                            (He puts needle against Thunderbolt's
                        backside and whacks it with mallet.)

                    Clang!

THUNDERBOLT   Ouch!

DOCTOR   Clang!

THUNDERBOLT   Ouch!

DOCTOR   Now, sir, you must be careful not to move. The needle
                    will come loose. Clang! Clang! Clang! Clang!

THUNDERBOLT   Ouch! Ouch! Ouch! Ouch! Quick, take it out! Take
                    it out!

DOCTOR   Indeed I will, sir.

                            (He takes out needle and goes back to
                        Sideman's spot.)

                    Ah, it worked.

THUNDERBOLT   What? You say it worked?

DOCTOR   Yes indeed.

                        (Thunderbolt gets up.)

THUNDERBOLT   Why, its marvelous! But there's still some pain right
                    here. Now put it in here.

DOCTOR   By all means, sir. Please lie down again.

THUNDERBOLT   Fine. Puff, grunt, groan.

     (This time he lies down facing no Chorus
    position. Doctor comes up to him.)

DOCTOR   This time, sir, you must try not to move the way you
        did a moment ago.

THUNDERBOLT Well then, you'd better stick it in so it doesn't
        hurt.

DOCTOR   Certainly, sir. Is it about here?

THUNDERBOLT Right, just about there.

DOCTOR   Then I'll knock it in, sir.

        (He repeats the business with the mallet.)

        Clang!

THUNDERBOLT Ouch!

DOCTOR   Clang!

THUNDERBOLT Ouch!

DOCTOR   Sir, please try not to move. Clang! Clang! Clang!
        Clang!

THUNDERBOLT Ouch! Ouch! Ouch! Ouch! Quick, take it out! Take
        it out!

DOCTOR   Indeed I will, sir.

        (As before, he takes out needle and goes
     to Sideman's spot.)

        Sir, it's out!

THUNDERBOLT You're sure?

DOCTOR   Absolutely, sir.

        (Thunderbolt gets up.)

        How do you feel?

THUNDERBOLT Wonderful! Just take my arm while I try to stand.

DOCTOR   Yes, sir. Now stand.

        (He goes up to Thunderbolt and takes his arm.)

THUNDERBOLT   Upsidaisy!

        (He stands up.)

DOCTOR   Are you all right, sir?

        (He goes back to Sideman's spot.)

THUNDERBOLT   My goodness me, you really are good. I feel wonderful again. Well, it's back up into the sky with me.

        (He goes toward mark post.)

DOCTOR   Oh, sir, do please wait a moment!

        (He rushes up to Thunderbolt and takes his sleeve.)

THUNDERBOLT   Wait? What do you mean?

DOCTOR   Please let me have my fee.

        (Doctor goes back to Sideman's spot; Thunderbolt is at mark post.)

THUNDERBOLT   Your fee?

DOCTOR   Sir, I'll explain. Each time I cure a human, he gives me an appropriate fee. Distinguished thunderbolt, please do the same!

THUNDERBOLT   That seems right enough. But I fell down here today so suddenly, I didn't bring a thing with me. I'll have to let you have these drumsticks.

DOCTOR   I don't need anything like that. Give me something else, sir.

THUNDERBOLT   Then I'll give you my drum.

DOCTOR   Sir, I'm not a child, a thing like that's no use to me. Do give me something else.

THUNDERBOLT   Goodness, what a problem! Then tell me where you live, and I'll drop back down and pay you.

DOCTOR	I'm afraid that's impossible, sir, I must have my fee here.
THUNDERBOLT	This really _is_ a pickle! What could I possibly do? Ah, most humans are full of wishes and desires. Don't you have a desire too?
DOCTOR	Now that you mention it, I do have a little wish.
THUNDERBOLT	What is it?
DOCTOR	They say a distinguished thunderbolt can do as he pleases with wind and rain. Is that true?
THUNDERBOLT	Certainly, I can do anything I like with them.
DOCTOR	You see, sir, when drought or flood strikes, ordinary people like me have a terrible time. Do please see to it that there are no floods or droughts.
THUNDERBOLT	That's fair enough. But how long should I keep it up?
DOCTOR	Forever, please.
THUNDERBOLT	No, no, that's too open-ended. I'll keep it up for you for a year.
DOCTOR	A year or two--any little dream lasts that long. How about watching against drought and flood for a thousand million years?
THUNDERBOLT	No, no, there's no end to a thousand million years. Ah, I know! This thunderbolt's got a brilliant idea! I'll watch for eight hundred years.
DOCTOR	I'm most grateful, sir.
THUNDERBOLT	And just for you, I'll pray that you get to be a Neurosurgeon.
DOCTOR	Oh sir, that would be wonderful!
THUNDERBOLT	Then I'll sing the whole thing and get on back up to the sky. You go over there and listen.

DOCTOR   By all means, sir.

         (He sits down right there. Thunderbolt
       is now before drums.)

THUNDERBOLT   Rain or shine

         (The Chorus, which a little while ago
       slipped in through slit door, now picks up the
       song from its position at back of stage. Thunder-
       bolt dances.)

CHORUS   rain or shine, eight hundred years shall we have

       free of drought or flood! An avatar you are of

       Yakushi in person! Great physician, you who heal

       dysphoria, you're a Neurosurgeon! cries he, and

       the Thunderbolt is up, up and away the Thunderbolt

       is up, up and away!

         (Thunderbolt chases Doctor around stage,
       bellowing.)

THUNDERBOLT   Wham, wham, zam, bang, bang, wham, zam, pow, kaboom!

         (Doctor, as Thunderbolt begins roaring, cries
       out and rushes around stage.)

DOCTOR   Ow! Mulberry! Mulberry!

         (He exits at a run, just ahead of Thunder-
       bolt. Chorus leaves by the slit door.)

MOUTH-OF-SOUND
(Eguchi: a woman play)

Now it is fall and the place is Eguchi, an old port on the Yodo
River near modern Osaka. Eguchi means the mouth of an inlet or es-
tuary, hence Mouth-of-Sound. However, the English title does contain
a double meaning not present in the Japanese.

The literary seed of Mouth-of-Sound, perhaps the noblest of
Kannami's surviving plays, is an exchange of poems between Saigyō
(1118-1190) and a harlot known as the Lady of Eguchi. Saigyō was a
monk, a wanderer, and a great poet. One rainy night, so the story
goes, he came into Eguchi and sought shelter at what happened to be a
house of assignation; there were not a few such houses in the little
port. The Lady, to whom it belonged, turned him away. Vexed at her
stinginess, he sent her a stinging poem; but in her reply she let him
know that she had been thinking only of his welfare. The point of the
exchange, which is included in the Shinkokinshū anthology, is the expression "passing shelter." This shelter is both the Lady's house
and the body in which the spirit of life momentarily dwells.

The theme of Mouth-of-Sound is the supposed contrast between
in-the-world and outside-the-world, and its resolution. In-the-world,
yo-no-naka, means 'life' as in "What a life!" or 'people' as in "What
will people say?" This inside/outside distinction is like that between 'at home' and 'abroad.' A Japanese monk is said to have 'left
home' or to have 'cast off the world.' But Mouth-of-Sound suggests
that there is an error here: it is not the body or the house that
are home, but the whole cosmos. This is something that Saigyō and the

Sideman should both know, but they need reminding.

The one who reminds them, the Lady, turns out at last to be the Bodhisattva Fugen. When Fugen rides up into the sky on her white elephant, one may be left wondering why the Bodhisattva is a woman here, and a harlot as well. The truth is that <u>she</u> is the whole cosmos.

Fugen is one of a pair of Bodhisattvas who accompany the Buddha himself; the other is Monju, who rides a lion. Roughly, Fugen is the Buddha's teaching and practice while Monju is his omniscient knowledge. Thus I see Monju as still and Fugen as evolving, in motion: form manifest. Now the Buddhist word for 'form' is translated into Chinese and Japanese with a character that also means 'color' and 'erotic desire.' Typically, a form is an object of desire and is naturally associated with the idea of beauty. And to represent the supreme object of desire, the supreme form, no better image could be found than that of a beautiful woman.

Japanese esoteric Buddhism (Shingon, the sect to which Saigyō belonged) names the sensible, consciously apprehendable, ever-evolving aspect of being <u>hosshin seppō</u>, the "preaching of the Dharmakaya." (The Dharmakaya is the universal Buddha not subject to space or time.) Thus whatever is manifest is the Buddha's teaching, i.e., sound; so that it is fitting for Fugen to appear not only as a lady, but as the Lady of Mouth-of-Sound.

But why is Fugen a harlot? Perhaps because, like beauty and enlightenment themselves, she is available to all. Desire for her may well enslave, but without her there is no liberation. In general Buddhism, a woman is definitely lower than a man, and a harlot is the lowest of the low. But as Komachi says in <u>Komachi on the Gravepost</u> (see the second volume of these translations), "Back links it is that lift one high"; by which she means that good children are not the ones who most swiftly soar beyond heaven.

The very symbol of enlightenment (which is beyond heaven as it is beyond hell) is the moon, and as the poetry of the play suggests, the Lady <u>is</u> the moon. As enlightenment or perfect wisdom, the moon is avowedly feminine, for the 'Wisdom Which Has Gone Beyond' is praised in Buddhist writings as 'the Mother of Bodhisattvas' who 'sets in motion the wheel of Dharma.' The moon, though, waxes and wanes, and the Lady is all phases. That is why she speaks of darkness as well as of light. No object of the senses or of consciousness, not even sin or despair, is outside the Teaching. Where indeed is "outside-the-world?"

SHIDAI	(Sideman and Sideman's Second enter. They face each other down front.)
SHIDAI on-w	
SIDEMAN AND SIDE SECOND	The moon long since has been my friend the moon long since has been my friend, so where's outside-the-world?
NANORI off	
SIDEMAN	(facing front) You have before you a monk who's come out of the district of the North. Lately I've been in Miyako, but I want to get on and take a look at all lands. First, then, I mean to go on pilgrimage to the mighty Buddhas and mighty shrines of the Inner Provinces. So, in the company of a few brothers, I'm off this very day.
AGEUTA on-w	
SIDEMAN AND SIDE SECOND	(face to face) Miyako still deep in night, we're off, the Yodo river craft runs down by Cormorant Hall's reeds vaguely glimpsed pines' smoking waves wash in to Mouth-of-Sound is where we've come Mouth-of-Sound is where we've come.
TSUKI- ZERIFU	
SIDEMAN	(facing front) This place we've reached is called the village of Mouth-of-Sound. Over there under those trees, beneath that banked rock seawall, I see a votive cairn. It looks like the relic of someone of consequence. I think I'll ask a local person.
	(Sideman's Second retires to near Sideman's spot. Sideman goes to main spot to call Fool, who is sitting at Fool's spot. Fool stands when addressed.)
MONDO off-sp	
	Hello! Is anyone around?

FOOL   Yes, what can I do for you?

SIDEMAN   Could you tell me the story of this votive cairn?

FOOL   This votive cairn marks the shade of the Lady of
            Mouth-of-Sound, a harlot who was famous in the old
            days. She was a poet, but the story goes that in
            fact she was an avatar of the Bodhisattva Fugen.
            Reverend Saigyo made a poem for her, to which, they
            say, she gave a lively reply. Men of heart comfort
            her. You should go there and do the same.

SIDEMAN   Thank you. I will.

                      (Fool sits again at Fool's spot. Sideman
                  faces front from center.)

   *
   off-w*
SIDEMAN   ᴴᴾ So, this is the shadow of the Lady of Mouth-of-
            Sound, of the old days. Her body is in earth, buried,
            but the name stays ˢ̠ till even now   long ago   though
            she lived   I call on her relic: a privilege indeed!
            ᴴᴾ Why, when Master Saigyo sought a night's lodging,
            ˢ̠ the house-owner   proved so heartless he sang,
            'The world and its ways   yes, are hard to scorn,
            And yet to cling   to passing shelter   most pleases
            you!'   And it was   this lady's shelter!   Ah, a
            witty poem!

                      (Sideman starts toward Sideman's spot.
                  Doer calls from behind the curtain, then enters,
                  wearing the zo-onna mask. While Sideman speaks,
                  she stops on bridgeway, facing front. Sideman
                  reaches Sideman's spot before he starts his speech.)

   MONDO
   off-w*
DOER   ᴴᴾ I beg your pardon, traveler! What moved you to
            sing that poem just now?

SIDEMAN   Strange! From over where there's no house to be seen,
            a woman has appeared; and she's asking about my singing

of the poem just now. Well, but why do you ask?

DOER   I'd forgotten   through the years   but again my
heart's tinged   with words' leaves of $\underline{s}$ grass
shaded fields,   a dewdrop world   yes, hard to
scorn   and yet to cling   to passing shelter . . .
The words shame me.   I did not cling,   and it's to
tell the story   I've come to you.

(She comes onstage and stands at main
spot.)

SIDEMAN $\underline{sp}$ I don't understand. '. . . to cling   to passing
shelter   most pleases you,' is what Saigyō sang for
the lady buried here. And just as I happen to be
comforting her, you protest to me that you didn't
cling to anything. Who are you?

DOER   No, but rather, I'm ashamed of what he must have
thought, to say, '. . . cling   to passing shelter.'
So why aren't you kind enough to sing the reply,
which says I did not cling?

SIDEMAN   Indeed, the words of the reply: $\underline{s}$ 'You despise the
world,

DOER   I gather, hence   set not your heart   on passing
shelter   is all I would say.' $\underline{sp}$ 'Set not your
heart,' I counseled him who'd cast off the world.
For I wouldn't have had him stay in a woman's house.
Wasn't that right?

SIDEMAN $\underline{?}$ Quite right, certainly. Saigyō himself   was one
who'd cast off   the passing shelter,

DOER   and I, a famous   lover of pleasure   whose dwelling
held   no few buried stumps, $\underline{s}$ things men disown;

SIDEMAN   set not your heart   went the song, for

DOER   my love went out to him   who'd renounced;

SIDEMAN   yet clinging

(Doer presses toward Sideman.)

DOER   was his own word--

        (Now she faces front. At 'never again,'
      she advances slightly; at 'set not,' turns to
      Sideman.)

  AGEUTA
  on-w

CHORUS   that I regret yet I cling to no passing shelter

       yet I cling to no passing shelter; why say I

       cling for evening waves never again return

       the old days, now set not your heart on worldly

       tales told by the unworldly.

  RONGI
  on-w

SIDEMAN AND   Indeed, a tale of the sad world indeed a tale
SIDE SECOND
       of the sad world; I listen while your very shape

       in twilight shadowed here dims out-- who can

       you be?

DOER   By twilight my stock-still form by twilight my

       stock-still form vaguely, vaguely glimmers, gone

       in river bends the Lady of the Stream of Mouth-

       of-Sound shows plain to see. I am ashamed!

        (Doer moves down to mark post, then turns
      left back up to main spot during following lines.)

SIDEMAN AND   Then there's no doubt: you are the shade who
SIDE SECOND
       faded out a wave on the wild shore!

DOER   'Here where a while I've made my home

SIDEMAN AND   the plum's tall sprays show up, no doubt--
SIDE SECOND

DOER   quite unlooked for

CHORUS   my lord, you've come!' A single tree sheltered

       us, surely, or perhaps we drew water from a

       single stream--imagine! and know me now,

> (She advances toward Sideman, opens;
> then turns right up to main spot, opens toward
> front.)

the phantom of   the Lady of Mouth-of-Sound,   voice

only   she is gone from sight   voice only   she is

gone from sight.

MONDO

> (Doer exits. Sideman now speaks to Fool,
> and tells him about the woman he has just seen.
> Fool says she must have been the phantom of the
> Lady of Mouth-of-Sound. He says he has heard that
> on moonlit nights the Lady can be seen in vision,
> and that at the end of the vision she may rise
> into the heavens, revealed as the Bodhisattva
> Fugen. Therefore, he says, the Sideman should
> wait and see. After Sideman thanks him, Fool exits.
> Sideman now stands at center.)

*
off-sp

SIDEMAN

Tramping around the lands as I do, I get to every

nook and cranny of the country; and that's how I can

witness such a wonder. No doubt it's thanks to my

merit in having left home to be a monk. Tonight the

whole   moonlit night through   by the relic of

the Lady of Mouth-of-Sound   I'll chant sutras;

> (During last phrase above, Sideman comes
> down front, while Sideman's Second stands and moves
> beside him. They face each other.)

AGEUTA
on-w

SIDEMAN AND
SIDE SECOND

and as I speak,   astonishing!   and as I speak,

astonishing!   On vast moon bright   river waters

harlot's songs resound,   their pleasure craft   shows

in the moon.   Ah, astonishing!

ISSEI

> (Sideman and Sideman's Second retire to
> Sideman's spot. Stagehand brings on the boat, a
> light framework roofed amidships where the Lady
> will stand, and places it at main spot. Doer now
> enters, wearing the zo-onna mask as before. A
> Second precedes her and another follows her, both
> wearing the tsure mask. They get into the boat.

                    The Second in the stern takes her outer robe off
                    her right shoulder and, holding an oar, mimes
                    sculling.)

AGEUTA
on-w

DOER, SECONDS   Our river craft   we halt to join   a rapid tryst

                  pillowed on waves   we halt to join   a rapid tryst

                  pillowed on waves;   the drifting world,   this

                  dream,   has dulled for us   who've seen it much,

                  we wonder not,   so cruelly fickle!   Where Lady

                  Sayo   pine-beach Strand   calls back to mind

                  sleeves spread forlorn   and wet with tears   for a

                  ship Cathay-bound;   and Uji too   where the Maiden

                  of the Bridge   pined for one   who would never

                  come.   Alas, the same lot   is our own!

SAGEUTA
on-w

                  Oh yes, Yoshino   oh yes, Yoshino's   blossoms and

                  snow   and clouds and waves   all, alas, foam   o

                  sorry world,   that one could join one's love!

KAKEAI
off-w*

SIDEMAN   <u>sp</u> With night quickly   deepening moon   on the

                  waters' face   floats a light craft,   and look!

                  within   harlots sing and sing: most seductive

                  human forms.   May I inquire   whose craft this is?

DOER   (turning to Sideman)   What?   This craft is   whose

                  craft, you ask?   Shameful to tell,   I of the old

                  days,   the harlot   of Mouth-of-Sound   sail the

                  stream   on the moon-bright   craft before you:

                  look then!

SIDEMAN   <u>s</u> Indeed!   Harlot   of Mouth-of-Sound,   you say--

                  why then,   are you the one   who in days of old . . .

DOER   No, by 'old days'   I mean how--See!   the moon ages

                  past   is quite unchanged!

SECONDS   We too here appear to you   not of the old days,
                 but fully real!

DOER   Well, let it be!   Ask what we are,

SECONDS   but we'll not say   or listen.

DOER   Ah, annoying talk!

    KAMI-NO-
    EI
    off-w

DOER, SECONDS   Waters of fall   brimming run down   and away goes
                 our craft   the moon rays dart   poling songs;

                         (Doer makes gestures to evoke the
                     Seconds' high spirits.)

    UTA
    on-w

CHORUS   sing on then, sing!   Bubbles of froth,   we'll tell,
                 alas,   our yearning love   for long ago   even now,
                 harlots   boating for pleasure   we'll cross over
                 life   with a measure of song.   Come, come, make
                 merry!

                         (During passage above, all get out of boat.
                     Seconds go to sit before Chorus, while Doer sits
                     before drums, on a stool provided by stagehand.
                     During passage below, stagehand removes the boat.)

    KURI
    off-w

CHORUS   Thus the Twelve Dependent Links revolve as a coach
                 turns round a park,

DOER   as birds sport in a wood;

CHORUS   past lives beyond past lives

DOER   till these lives' first past   lies beyond all knowing;

CHORUS   future births on future births,   and where these
                 births shall end   there is no telling.

    SASHI
    off-w

DOER   Some receive the Good Fruits which are the realms of
             Men or Heaven

CHORUS   but, distracted and confused,   still plant no Seed
             of Liberation.

DOER   Some fall in the Evil Paths   of the Three Ways,
             the Eight Pains,

CHORUS   and, barred by anguish,   lose all help toward
             Aspiration.

DOER   Yet though we chance to have human bodies,   always
             hard to gain,

CHORUS   we were born deep in evil karma   to become, a thing
             most rare,   river bamboo women of the stream.   Oh,
             painful it is to ponder   this our reward for lives
             gone by!

                          (Doer checks tears, then stands. Below, at
                          'woods,' she gazes around while with fan indicating
                          the panorama; at 'burst,' does leftright to mark
                          pause; at 'fall winds,' comes down front; at 'once
                          gone,' advances two steps; at 'pillows,' points at
                          head with fan; at 'plants and trees,' goes to mark
                          post, then sweeps left to center; at 'evade,' does
                          leftright to mark pause, then spreads fan; at
                          'stained,' strikes fan high pose; at 'hear a voice,'
                          moves down front with a full leftright; at 'Six
                          Dusts,' moves right up to main spot, then goes
                          down to mark post, then displays fan as she sweeps
                          left up to drums; there she concludes dance with a
                          leftright.)

   KUSE
   on-w

CHORUS   In scarlet blossoming   spring's own morning   scarlet
             brocaded hills   deck themselves   before our eyes,
             yet evening winds   lure all away   the golden leaves
             in fall,   while at dusk   forest's golden   tie-dyed
             stuffs   burst with color,   in next morning's frost
             they shift and fade.   As fall winds tinge   moonlit
             vines,   handsome guests   gently converse;   they
             too once gone   will come no more.   Hung round

with green   in scarlet chamber   lovers lay   their
pillows twinned;   they too soon   will go their
ways.   Yes, plants and trees   that have no heart,
human beings,   gifted with feeling: which of these
shall evade sorrow?   So we reflect,

DOER

yet are at times   stained with love's hue,   harbor
desires   by no means shallow;

CHORUS

or at times   we hear a voice   and love's yearning
runs very deep.   The heart's fond pangs,   the
mouth's own words,   turn to links   with wrongful
clinging.   Alas, all men wander, lost,   the Realm
of the Six Dusts,   and commit sins   of the Six Sense
Roots,   for all things seen,   all things heard,
turn to the heart's confusion.

WAKA
off-w

Astonishing!

JO-NO-
MAI

(Doer withdraws a moment to Doer post, then
begins a jo-no-mai dance. As text resumes, she is
at main spot in fan high pose.)

WAKA
w

DOER

off Astonishing!   On the great sea   of True Phase
Perfectly Contained,   winds of the Five Dusts   and
the Six Desires   do never blow,

CHORUS

onori yet waves of True Semblance   Linked in Sequence
rise each and every day   rise each and every day.

(Doer moves toward mark post; then,
chanting the while, sweeps left up to drums.)

*
off-w

DOER

And the waves rise   for what reason, pray?   We set
our heart

NORIJI
onori-w

on passing shelter.

>   (She moves to center. At 'lovers,' she
> opens, then, displaying fan, moves to mark post;
> at 'parting,' looks up, then moves to center and
> glances to left and right; at 'utterly,' turns
> right up to main spot and claps hands.)

CHORUS   Did we not so,   no sad world would be,

DOER   no lovers yearn;

CHORUS   no nights of pining,

DOER   no parting of ways   storm swept

CHORUS   blossoms! red maples!   moon and snow falling

                through all old songs   ah, utterly fruitless!

>   (Below, at second 'indeed,' Doer stamps
> several beats; at 'set not,' points fan at Sideman
> and advances toward him, gazing intently; at 'it is
> over,' moves down front; at 'All-Wise,' strikes
> Excitement pose; at 'her craft,' looks down and
> points around her with fan, then moves to mark
> post; at 'she mounts,' sweeps left, stamps beat,
> proceeds to main spot; at first 'grateful,' opens
> toward front, then turns toward side.)

    UTA
    on-w

DOER   Yes indeed   a passing shelter

CHORUS   yes indeed   a passing shelter--   there set not your

                heart,   the man was warned,   and by me!   It is

                over,   now I go,   says she;   and instantly   All-

                Wise Fugen   the Bodhisattva   stands revealed.   Her

                craft now turns   white elephant,   glory attends her

                as she mounts   the white clouds'   candid brightness,

                rides off   to the western skies.   What grateful

                joy   she has inspired,   oh what grateful joy!

>   (Facing side, Doer stamps final beat.)

PINING WIND
(Matsukaze: a woman play)

In Pining Wind, the mood of autumn deepens. This play about
love's unquenchable longing is wonderfully moving even if one hardly
'understands' it at all: it is a fine example of how a pattern, once
traced, can be apprehended in many ways. Together with "Yuya,"
Pining Wind is traditionally the most popular play of all. Both together have been called what amounts to the actor's bread and butter.

Pining Wind was apparently written by Kannami, then reworked by
Zeami. Though the story is found nowhere else, Yukihira, Pining
Wind's beloved, did in fact exist. He lived from 818 to 893, and was
a brilliant courtier and poet. Yukihira's older brother, Narihira,
is Yukihira's counterpart in The Well Cradle. Yukihira may actually
have been exiled to Suma, a section of shore not far from the modern
Kōbe, and certainly the fictional hero Prince Genji spent several
melancholy years there. Pining Wind often echoes the Suma chapter
of the Tale of Genji. Prince Genji too had a purification rite per-
formed at Suma on the day of the Serpent, early in the third moon of
the year.

It is possible to translate the name Pining Wind because the
same double meaning exists both in English and in Japanese: matsu
means 'to wait' and 'pine tree.' Thus, 'pining wind' really has four
meanings: wind blowing through pine boughs; the wind's sound; wind
that waits in longing; and finally (taking 'to pine' as a verb that
means 'to be a pine') wind that is a pine. This last meaning is
danced out near the end of the play.

Pining Wind has told in full her love for the long dead Yukihira
and has evoked his presence by putting on, as though compelled, the
hat and cloak he left her as keepsakes. She has impersonated him.
Now, unable to do more, she collapses in despair and sings of Three
Shallows River (Mitsusegawa), the river that surrounds the underworld;
her spirit has sunk down to hell. But as the lowest leads to the
highest, Pining Wind raises her head again to see Yukihira (a pine
tree) standing before her in the flesh. He is as much a 'Vert Galant'
as the God of Sumiyoshi in Takasago, and he has come instantly, as he
promised he would, to Pining Wind's cry of total yearning. When
Pining Wind dances around him, she in her human form is wearing his
clothes, while he in his pine form sings the song which is of her,
the wind. He really is a 'wind-bent pine.' As the moon is the
visible sign of wisdom, so the pining wind is the audible sign, or
pattern, of divine love.

As Yukihira and Pining Wind merge, so do their colors. Near the
start of the play, the Sideman says, 'A pine, one lone tree, leaves a
green fall.' ('A pine, one lone tree' is matsu hito ki, which can
also mean 'the pining one comes.')   One sees a pine standing green
amid the changing colors of fall, especially the reds and golds of
the momiji, the maple leaves--for maple leaves are as much the mark
of fall in Japan as in New England. Pining Wind's dance around the
tree is the same picture, for her color is that of expanding energy,
of burning, of love. Red is indeed the color of a beautiful woman in
nō, and the costume for such a role is said to 'contain red.'

Sudden Rain, the Second, also has an eloquent name. In Japanese,

<u>murasame</u> means a quick, hard shower. So unlike Pining Wind, who is
continuous, Sudden Rain is stop-and-start. She forgets while Pining
Wind remembers. Appropriately, it is she who introduces the Sideman
into the salt shed, and again she, not the pining wind, who disappears
in the end. The dialogue between Pining Wind and Yukihira really
goes on forever; it is Sudden Rain who is the passing storm which is
the play. She is like a sudden whitecap that opens one's eyes to
the whole rolling sea.

Salt-making, the livelihood of Pining Wind and Sudden Rain, is
often mentioned in poetry, and in fact the play contains a <u>tsukushi</u>,
or 'inventory,' of places associated with salt-making. (Another
'inventory,' on trees, will be found in <u>The Golden Tablet</u>.) Such a
passage means relatively little, but plays a great deal with pun and
allusion. It is like a rocky section of stream which effectively
prepares one to appreciate the smoother flow beyond. As for salt-
making itself, the process it involved (gathering seaweed, pouring
brine over it, roasting it, steeping the roasted seaweed in more
brine, then finally drawing the liquid off and boiling it down) was
more complicated than one might expect.

(A small pine stands down front.

SHIDAI   Sideman enters and stands at main spot, facing back
       of stage.)

SHIDAI
on-w

SIDEMAN   Suma, Akashi along those shores Suma, Akashi
       along those shores the moon and I we'll wander
       forth!

NANORI
off-sp

       (facing front) You have before you a brother who's
       taking a look at all lands. Lately I've been in
       Miyako, where I've seen each scenic spot and ancient
       relic of noble Rakuyō. Now, I've decided to tramp
       on to the lands of the West.

TSUKI-
ZERIFU
off-sp

       Hurrying along that way, here I am all right in the
       land of Tsu at Suma shore, or some such place.

         (He notices the pine and moves toward it.)

       Remarkable! Right here on the beach there's a
       striking pine. This pine undoubtedly has a history.
       I think I'll ask one of the local people.

         (He goes to main spot. Fool is sitting
       at Fool's spot, and stands up when called.)

MONDO
off-sp

       Hello! Is anyone around?

FOOL   What can I do for you?

SIDEMAN   I beg your pardon, but I'm very struck by this pine
       here on the shore. Can you tell me anything about
       it?

FOOL   Well, I'm afraid I'm very ignorant when it comes to
       things like that. But from what I've heard, that

pine marks a grave: the grave of two seafolk named
Pining Wind and Sudden Rain. It certainly would be
kind of you if you'd raise them and pray before you
pass on.

SIDEMAN   Then I'll do so. Thank you.

FOOL   At your service.

                        (Fool exits. Sideman moves to center,
                 facing pine.)

    *
    off-w*

SIDEMAN   <u>s</u> So, this pine long ago was   Pining Wind, Sudden
                 Rain   so-called, two seafolk's   ancient relic.   A
                 sad, sad story!   Their bodies are in earth buried
                 but the names linger   now, for their sign   unchanging
                 in hue   a pine, one lone tree   leaves a green fall.
                 Ah, most moving!   <u>sp</u> Now that I've prayed that way
                 with sutras and invocations to Amida, well, it's just
                 as you'd expect on a fall day: in no time the sun's
                 gone down.   That hamlet at the foot of the mountains
                 is a long way off, so I think I'll go up to this
                 seafolk's salt shed and see the night through here.

                        (Sideman retires to Sideman's spot.
SHIN-NO-   Stagehand brings on the brine scoop wagon, repre-
ISSEI   sented by a small, light framework prop, and places
                 it at base of mark post. One bucket is loaded on
                 it. Now Second enters, wearing the <u>tsure</u>, or
                 Second, mask, and carrying another bucket. She is
                 followed by Doer, wearing the <u>wakaonna</u>, or Young
                 Woman, mask. Second stops at first pine, Doer at
                 third pine. They face each other.)

ISSEI
off-w

DOER, SECOND   A brine scoop wagon   wheels meagerly   the sorry
                 world   round and round   so cruelly fickle!

SECOND   (facing front) Waves right at our feet   on Suma
                 shore

DOER, SECOND   (again face to face)   the very moon soaks   a trailing sleeve.

                    (Second now moves to center, Doer to main spot. They face front.)

SASHI
off-w

DOER   Hearts empty   in the fall wind   so while the sea was somewhat far

DOER, SECOND   (face to face)   noble Yukihira   the Middle Counsel sang '. . . blows through the pass'   where the curved shore waves   surge nigh each night   sounding so near   the seafolk's home;   the hamlet's far   down our path to and fro   beside the moon   there's no company.

DOER   Yes, the sad world's   work does claim us   but utterly wretched   the seafolk's craft   that makes no way   over life, this dream   where 'I live' is no word   for a bubble of froth   on the brine   scoop wagon   without safe haven   for us, the seafolk whose sleeves together   with yearning love   the heart never lets dry!

                    (They face front.)

SAGEUTA
on-w

CHORUS   'So thoroughly   does all life seem   hard to pass through'   that in envy   we dwell   on the clear moon's   rising tide, come, scoop!

                    (Doer steps forward.)

Scoop the rising tide!

                  (Noticing her reflection, she lowers her head. At 'lingering,' she stares into water again; at 'in the sun,' looks to her right as though gazing along the shore; at first 'shrivel,' retreats to main spot and expresses grief.)

AGEUTA
on-w

    This image shames me   my own form   this image
    shames me   my own form   shrinks low, a wain   drawn
    withdrawing tides   leave lingering pools   how long
    to live on?   Yes, on meadow grasses   dewdrops in
    the sun   dwindle and vanish   but on the pebbled
    shore   sea wrack-raking seafolk   cast weeds all
    a-tangle   to shrival, wilting   trailing sleeves
    shrivel, wilting   trailing sleeves.

SASHI
off-w

DOER   How lovely!   though so familiar,   Suma at dusk:
    seafolk's cries   come faint

DOER, SECOND   (face to face)   offshore   little fishing craft
    show dim   the moon's full face,   silhouetted wild
    geese,   flocking plovers,   cutting gales, salt
    winds,   yes, each one   in such a place means fall;
    oh, the heart-chilling   long night hours!

KAKEAI
off-w

DOER   Come, come!   Let's scoop brine!   she says   at the
    sea's edge   flood and ebb   tides salty clothes,

SECOND   sleeves we tie   drape on the shoulder

DOER   to scoop brine   or so we hope

SECOND   but hold!   try as we may

DOER   a woman's wagon

AGEUTA
on-w

CHORUS   rolled in falls back   single breakers   roll in fall
    back   single waves;

        (Above, Second retreats to drums while Doer
    goes toward mark post. Now Doer gazes into distance
    to her right; at 'storm blasts,' she faces front;
    at 'live it through,' lowers head in dejection; at
    'deepening moon,' gazes up to her right at moon; at
    'our scoops,' shifts gaze to wagon.)

out by the reeds   cranes start up crying,   all
four storm blasts   add their roar;   night's icy
cold,   how'll we live it through?   The deepening
moon   shines so bright!   Our scoops catch   the
reflection!   Salt fire smoke: watch out for that!
This is the way   we seafolk   shall live out gloomy
fall.

> (Doer kneels on one knee beside the wagon;
> at 'scoops,' uses fan to mime ladling brine into
> bucket, while gazing at moon's reflection within.)

SAGEUTA
on-w

CHORUS   Pine Island's   Hero Island's seafolk   beneath the
moon   scoop reflections, ah,   with keen delight
scoop reflections, ah,   with keen delight!

> (Doer returns to main spot.)

RONGI
on-w

A long haul's theirs   far up north   in Michinoku
where the name's Near   Chika, and Shiogama Salt
Kilns . . .

DOER   'Humble men   hauled salt wood . . .'--   on Akogi
coast it was   withdrawing tides . . .

CHORUS   Yes, the same Ise sea has   Futami, Twin Glance, shore,
and it's twice   I'd go out in the world!

DOER   Pine groves stand   hazy glows the sun   as tide
roads, far, far out   sound past Narumigata,   Bight
of the Sounding Sea;

CHORUS   yonder's Narumigata,   here at Naruo   beneath the
pines   moonlight's blocked off   by Reedy Roofs   of
Ashinoya.

DOER   Scooping brine   from Nada Channel's   a sad life,
though   tell none willow comb

CHORUS   thrust in combing tides   scoop down and   look!

                   the moon   right in my pail!

                            (Above at 'thrust,' Second approaches wagon
                   and places her bucket on it. Doer stares into
                   buckets from where she stands. Now, Doer advances
                   a little; Second hands her the cord for pulling the
                   wagon, then goes to main spot. At 'moon is one,'
                   Doer gazes aloft, then back to wagon; at 'for
                   tonight,' she pulls wagon up to drums, then turns
                   round and gazes into buckets once more; at 'tide
                   roads,' stamps beat.)

DOER   In mine too   the moon's slipped in!

CHORUS   Oh lovely!   Here too the moon!

DOER   Moon is one

CHORUS   reflections two   three the brimming tide   for

                   tonight our wagon's   loaded with the moon.   Sad?

                   Why, not at all,   the tide roads of the sea!

                            (Stagehand removes the wagon. Doer sits on
                   a stool before drums, facing front; Second sits in
                   the ordinary way a little behind her and to her
                   right. They are in the salt shed. Sideman stands
                   and faces them.)

    MONDO
    off-w*

SIDEMAN   <u>sp</u> Excuse me, there in the salt shed! I beg your

                   pardon!

                            (Second stands and advances a little toward
                   Sideman.)

SECOND   What is it?

SIDEMAN   I'm traveling through, and the sun's gone down on me.
                   I'd appreciate shelter for the night.

SECOND   Please wait a moment. I'll ask the owner.

                            (She kneels on one knee before Doer. Hence-
                   forth she moves thus between Doer and Sideman, as
                   appropriate.)

                   Excuse me, but a traveler has come. He says he'd like

shelter for the night.

DOER That's a simple request, no doubt, but this place isn't
fit to be seen. Please tell him we really can't let
him stay.

SECOND I asked the owner, who says that as this place isn't
fit to be seen, we really can't let you stay.

SIDEMAN I quite understand. But if the place isn't fit to be
seen, it certainly won't bother me. I'm a wandering
monk, after all. So I do ask you again: please allow
me to see the night through here.

SECOND The traveler is a monk, and he insists on asking again
for a night's shelter.

DOER What! You say the traveler's a monk? ^s— By the moon's
night shine I see one who's cast off the world; well,
it will do, this seafolk's home with posts of pine
and bamboo fence. The night's cold, I know; tell him
to warm himself at our rush fire and stay.

SECOND Do please come in.

SIDEMAN Ah, with pleasure!

> (Sideman advances a few steps and sits,
> while Second returns to her place. They are in
> the shed.)

MONDO
off-w*

DOER <u>sp</u> From the start I wanted to put you up. But this
place isn't fit to be seen, and that's why I refused.

SIDEMAN Thank you for your kindness. I've always been a monk
and a wanderer, and it's not mine to settle anywhere.
So how should I choose my shelter? Certainly, here
on Suma shore, any sensitive person ought actually to
prefer a rather melancholy life: <u>s</u> 'Should one by
chance   inquire for me,   say I'm at Suma shore;
<u>sp</u> say the tangle-salt drips down   and I am sad.'
Yes, that's what Yukihira himself sang. By the way,

when I saw that lone pine over there on the shore,
I asked a fellow about it. He said something about
it being an ancient relic of two seafolk named Pining
Wind and Sudden Rain. Of course they're nothing to
me, but I did comfort them and pray before I went on.

(Doer and Second both hide tears.)

DOER, SECOND   <u>s</u> Oh, it's true!   When love's within,   love's hues
show without!   The way you quoted,   'Should one
by chance   inquire for me,'   gave such pangs of
longing!   And tears of Jambudvīpa,   the world of
clinging,   wet our sleeves once more.

(They both weep.)

MONDO
off-sp

SIDEMAN   Tears of Jambudvīpa, the world of clinging? You talk
like people who've left this life! And the poem
'Should one by chance' gives you pangs of longing, or
so I gather. It's all very strange. Both of you,
name yourselves!

KUDOKI-
GURI
off-w

DOER, SECOND   I'm ashamed!   Let me begin to tell,   and should one
by chance   inquire after me,   he'd vanish, a
shadow   world where salt-drenched   I learn no lesson
but ever assume a   surely bitter heart!

KUDOKI
off-w

After all this,   what need we   so carefully conceal?
We are . . .   This twilight past   you kindly raised
two vanished shades   up from the moss   beneath that
pine,   Pining Wind, Sudden Rain,

(They turn to Sideman.)

two girls' darkened spirits   have come to you here.

Yes, Yukihira   a full three years   lightened his
leisure   with pleasant boating;   the moon cleared
his heart   on Suma shore.   While we hauled the night
brine   with seafolk maidens   he courted and chose
us.   'What perfect names   for now!' he said   and
deigned to call us   Pining Wind, Sudden Rain.
The moon we knew well,   we Suma seafolk.

DOER   but saltburner's clothes   were all transformed

DOER, SECOND   to stiff silk summer robes   censed with sweet
                fragrance.

DOER   So three years flew;   then Yukihira   went up to our
                Sovereign's Seat.

SECOND   He'd no sooner gone   than this life, so young,

DOER, SECOND   he departed: so we heard.

DOER   And ever since,   oh, I've missed him so!   Still,
                perhaps   in another life   he'll come calling

    UTA
    on-w

CHORUS   pining   Wind and Sudden Rain   drench these sleeves
                helpless, alas,   with love far beyond us.   The Suma
                seafolk   are deep in sin:

                        (They bow to Sideman with palms joined.)

                kindly, brother,   raise our shadows!

                        (They turn front again.   At second 'dew,'
                    Second goes to sit before Chorus, while Sideman
                    retires to Sideman's spot; at 'melt away,' Doer
                    looks down, showing deep emotion.)

    AGEUTA
    on-w

                Love's grasses grow   dew, passions   all tangled
                dew, passions   all tangled;   the heart's madness
                wears dear   easy robes.   The Day of the Serpent
                brings a blessing!   Mulberry streamers   to ask the

gods' help   wave on useless   wave-borne froth   we
grieve and melt away   to lasting sorrow!

> (After opening words of the passage below,
> stagehand gives Doer a length of cloth to represent
> the cloak, and an <u>eboshi</u> hat. At 'each time,' Doer
> lifts them up and gazes at them; at 'blade tips,'
> she gazes at ends of her own sleeves; at 'his keep-
> sakes,' lifts them high again; at 'someone sang,'
> lowers them and checks tears; at 'on and on,' stands,
> still holding hat and cloak, and goes to mark post;
> at 'fruitless,' throws them down, but instantly picks
> them up again and holds them close; at 'standing,
> lying,' turns to her right up to main spot, then
> looks back toward bridgeway as though pursued by a
> power; at 'sink down,' collapses, weeping, to a
> sitting position.)

KUSE
on-w

CHORUS   Alas!   When I recall the past   I miss him so!   Yukihira   the Middle Counsel   three years dwelt   on
Suma shore,   then went up to   our Sovereign's Seat.
'Some keepsakes of these days!'   he said   and kindly
left us   a tall court hat,   a hunting cloak.   Each
time I see them   ever more   passion grasses spring;
the blade tips bear   dewdrops gone   so soon might I
forget,   oh, wretched agony!   'His keepsakes, yes,
are now my foe: without them   a forgetful pause
might come,'   so someone sang: very true!   More and
more my love   deepens in power.

DOER   Dusk after dusk   before I sleep   I shed the hunting
habit,

CHORUS   put it on   and on I beg   that in one same world . . .
Life is empty,   I can't forget   these fruitless
keepsakes!   She throws them down   but cannot leave
them,   takes them up   and his shape looms.   Standing
lying   are the same: 'From the pillow,   from the
bed's foot   love comes against me;'   helpless,
weeping   I sink down   in utter misery.

>   (Stagehand approaches Doer, drapes the
>   cloak over her and places the hat on her head.
>   Below, Doer checks tears.)

SHIMO-
NO-EI
off-weak

DOER   Three Shallows River: endless tears,   that unhappy
        shoal,   hold, yes, even they,   a gulf of churning
        love.

>   (She looks up.)

KAKEAI
off-w*

        $\underline{s}$ Oh, what happiness! Yukihira's standing right over
        there!

>   (She stands and moves toward pine.)

        'Pining Wind!' he's calling! I'm going to him!

>   (Second quickly stands, grasps Doer's
>   right sleeve. At 'crazed longing,' Doer goes to
>   drums, Second retreats toward side.)

SECOND   How awful! It's just the state you're in now that
         sinks one in the sin of clinging. You still haven't
         escaped the crazed longing you felt when you belonged
         to the world! That's a pine tree. Yukihira just
         isn't there.

DOER $\underline{sp}$ You're unsteady   to talk that way!   That pine
         $\underline{is}$ Yukihira! $\underline{s}$ Though for a while   we may be
         parted,   tell me you're pining   and I'll come back:
         so he sang for us--   now what do you say?

SECOND   You're right! I'd completely forgotten! Though for
         a while   we may be parted,   pine and I'll come:
         those were the words

DOER   I'd not forgotten   pining   wind's up now   he's
         coming home,   his message

SECOND   one day may touch   sudden rain   to wet these sleeves
         a while, surely

DOER   pining as ever   he's coming home,

SECOND   we trusted rightly

DOER   his dear poem:

   WAKA
   off-w

DOER, SECOND   'I'm up to leave you,

                    (Hiding tears, Doer runs toward bridgeway;
             Second, crying too, goes to sit before Chorus.
   CHU-NO-   Doer runs back onstage from first pine, stopping at
   MAI   main spot. She then does a chu-no-mai dance. At
             last, as she resumes the singing of the poem, she
             strikes fan high pose.)

   WAKA
   off-w

bound away   for Inaba's mountain   peaks so green

with   pining's needless: call me   and it's now

I'll be home.'

                    (Below, at 'yonder,' Inaba,' Doer gazes into
             distance toward bridgeway; at 'here my longing,'
             comes to center, pointing at pine with fan; at
             'curved shore,' sweeps fan around, indicating an
             expanse of sea; at 'back with me,' turns right up
             to drums; at 'by the tree,' glides down to the
             pine; at 'love him still,' retreats, weeping, back
             to drums.)

   NORIJI
   onori-w

DOER   Yonder, Inaba's   far mountain pines

CHORUS   here my longing   my beloved Lord here   on Suma's

                curved shore   pines Yukihira   back with me   while

                by the tree   I rise now, draw near   so dear   the

                wind bent pine,   I love him still!

   HO-NO-
   MAI   (Doer stops weeping, lifts her head   and
             dances round and round the tree. This ha-no-mai
             dance is brief, but spirited. As text resumes, she
             moves to center, making beckoning gestures; at
             'mighty waves,' sweeps fan around and gazes out
             over sea; at 'clinging,' turns right up to main
             spot; then moves to center, kneels facing Sideman
             and joins palms in prayer; at 'good-bye,' stands,

stamps beat; at 'Suma shore,' goes to mark post
and strikes clasped fan pose while gazing toward
mountains in the direction of the flute post; at
'cocks,' moves downstage from Sideman's spot,
strikes cloud fan pose and gazes into sky; at
'you heard indeed,' goes to main spot; at first
'pining wind,' opens toward front, then faces
side and stamps final beat.)

NORIJI
onori-w

CHORUS   Pining the tree-bound   wind turns mad,   Suma's

mighty waves   rage the night through;   wrongful

clinging dreams   us for you, kindly,   raise our

shadows!   Good-bye we say   retreating waves sound

UTA   clear down Suma shore   blows the back hills'   seaward

on-w   breeze;   the pass road's where   cocks are crowing,

the dream is gone   without a shadow   night opens

into dawn.   Sudden rain   you heard indeed   but

this morning see,   pining wind is all   that lingers

pining wind alone   lingers on.

KOMACHI AT GATEWAY TEMPLE
(Sekidera Komachi: a woman play
or a miscellaneous play)

Komachi at Gateway Temple takes place on the seventh night of
the seventh moon of the year. This is the night of Tanabata, a
festival which is still celebrated in Japan. Nowadays Tanabata is on
the night of July 7, in the height of summer. In the lunar calendar,
however, the seventh day of the seventh moon falls several weeks
later, at the start of fall. A month in the solar calendar is not
the same as a 'moon.' Nor indeed was an 'hour' in pre-modern Japan
the same as one of our hours. Day and night were divided into six
periods each, no matter what the season, so that each period waxed and
waned in length through the year.

On Tanabata, or Seventh Night, the two celestial lovers meet:
the Herd-Boy star (Altair) crosses the River of Heaven (the Milky Way)
to the Weaver star (Vega) over a bridge formed of the joyously-linked
wings of magpies. In this play, a celebration is being offered at
Gateway Temple for the occasion. There is to be music and dancing,
and many bamboo wands tied with streamers of five colors. These wands
are prayer sticks, to pray for various blessings including skill in
poetry.

To hear more about poetry, some priests and children from the
temple go to visit an old lady who lives nearby. She turns out to
be Ono no Komachi, who in her youth was a peerless beauty and a great
poet. Now she is only a year short of one hundred, the forgotten ruin
of a woman.

The historical Ono no Komachi was active in the mid-ninth century,

and left behind her a vivid legend. There is no other record of her
having retired to Gateway Temple, below the eastern slope of Osaka
Pass, but it is fitting that at the gates of death, she should live
in such a place. Osaka Pass was indeed the gateway from Miyako toward
what were in Komachi's time the wilds of the east and north, and it
was famous for painful separations.

Several passages of Komachi at Gateway Temple are taken from the
preface to the Kokinshū, which was the canonical statement on poetry.
It is this preface which singles out the 'Naniwa Harbor' and 'Mount
Asaka' poems for special comment. Naniwa was a port on the site of
modern Osaka, and the poem goes, 'At Naniwa Harbor it blooms! this
flower winter-long shut in, now spring is here it blooms! this flower.'
The 'Mount Asaka' poem can be roughly translated: 'Mount Asaka, re-
flecting you the rocky pool's shallow this heart is not in desire.'
The ancient story goes that when the King of Kazuraki visited northern
Japan, he felt poorly received and refused to eat or drink until a
serving girl came up to him with a full wine cup, tapped him on the
knee, and recited this verse; everything went smoothly from then on.
It is also the Kokinshū preface that describes Komachi's poetry as
'affecting, but not strong.'

Komachi at Gateway Temple mentions 'cloud walkers,' meaning the
nobles of the imperial court, for the Emperor's own palace is known
as the 'cloud dwelling.' Figuratively speaking, all of Japan was one
mountain, on top of which was the Imperial Seat--this is the meaning
of the word miyako which became the common name for the Capital. One
always traveled 'up' to Miyako, and 'down' from it.

Komachi at Gateway Temple is held to be the loftiest play in the
repertoire, and only a senior and distinguished actor would dare to
perform its main role. Some say the role is so difficult and so lofty
because Komachi does not move at all during the first hour or so of
the play--as though loftiness were measured by the obligation to tol-
erate, toward some esoteric end, intolerable boredom. There is some
truth in this, but surely the real loftiness comes from the play's
transparent simplicity of tone. There are masterpieces, but this is
a past-masterpiece, beyond praise. Zeami, who may possibly have
written it, says that an old actor who has truly mastered the 'flower'
of the art will always be perfectly fresh even though he is long past
the age for brilliance. His acting will be like blossoms on an old
bough. In Komachi at Gateway Temple, this image is applied to Komachi
herself, as she dances at last. The whole play, though, is actually
like that. Beside an old, old woman whose age has brought her out of
the world into a second innocence, one sees the children, dressed in
their best, gravely dancing for the Stars.

SHIDAI	(Komachi's hut stands before drums. From it hang a few slips of paper for writing poems. Sideman and Sideman's Second enter, preceded by Child. They line up down front, with Sideman and Sideman's Second facing each other.)
SHIDAI on-str	
SIDEMAN AND SIDE SECOND	The waiting ends now fall's rejoined the waiting ends now fall's rejoined the Stars: hasten their feast!
NANORI off-sp	
SIDEMAN	(facing front) You have before you the head priest of Gateway Temple in the land of Ōmi. Today being the seventh day of the seventh month, we're all going into the garden of the Lecture Hall, to celebrate Seventh Night. But now, an old woman has put together a hut under this mountain, and I understand she's a master of the Way of Song; so I'm taking the young people with me to hear what she has to say.
SASHI off-str	
SIDEMAN AND SIDE SECOND	(face to face) 'Hiss and sigh the chilling winds and wilting hairs converge at start of fall,' and evening of the seventh day so soon has come.
SIDEMAN	(facing front) This Seventh Night we've offerings: strings, pipes tuned to modes and scales many-hued words urge we forth for Blessed Isles'
AGEUTA on-str	
SIDEMAN AND SIDE SECOND	(face to face) Way our prayer threads streaming bright Way our prayer threads streaming bright oh, weave brocade loom the flags of pampas grasses, flowers too and autumn weeds dew-spangled sing, so gently plays the pining wind,

(Sideman takes a few steps and returns to
his place by start of next passage.)

itself perfect   offering   this wondrous night

offering   this wondrous night!

**TSUKI-
ZERIFU**
off-sp

SIDEMAN   (facing front)   You wait here a moment, while I
inquire within the hut.

> (All go to sit near Sideman's spot. Stage-
> hand removes cover from the hut, revealing Doer
> seated inside. She wears the rojo, or Old Woman,
> mask.)

SASHI
off-w

DOER   Though mornings I get not one bowl, seek food I
cannot;   though grass wraps, nights, hide not my
flesh I have nothing more.   Flowers, as rains go by,
lose their scarlet youth;   willows, as breezes lure
them, let the green fronds droop.   Man is not young
again: at last he's old,   and though spring come
with warblers'   hundred carolings,   no fall goes
back   to yesteryear.   Oh the old days,   I miss
them so!

> (She gently checks tears.)

Oh the old days,   I miss them so!

> (Sideman stands, and has Child stand also.)

MONDO
off-w*

SIDEMAN   <u>sp</u> Old lady, I beg your pardon, but I'd like to
speak with you.

DOER   Who is it?

SIDEMAN   I'm from Gateway Temple. The children of the temple
are studying poetry, and they've been asking about
the old lady. So I've brought them along to ask you
how to compose songs, and to listen to whatever you
have to say.

(Sideman and Child move closer to Doer.)

DOER   You do astonish me! A buried stump disowned by men, that's what I am: no longer shall plumed pampas grass burst into fruit. Just make the heart your seed, and dip the flowers of your speech in hue and fragrance. If you do, then how should you fail to grasp true style? (turning to Child) How lovely that all this should appeal to you young people!

SIDEMAN   One that everyone praises right off is the 'Naniwa Harbor' song, and I understand it's to be considered the first model for learners. Isn't that so?

DOER   Very definitely. Song, you see, began in the Age of Gods, but the count of letters then kept changing, and likely enough the heart of the matter was difficult to make out. Now we're in the Age of Men; and it's because the poem celebrates a happy Imperial accession that people make much of the 'Naniwa Harbor' song.

SIDEMAN   And the 'Mount Asaka' song is a very happy poem too, since it soothed the heart of a king!

DOER   Yes, you understand perfectly. With these two songs as mother and father

SIDEMAN $\underline{s}$ and first model for all learners,

DOER $\underline{sp}$ men high and low, of all degrees,

SIDEMAN $\underline{s}$ town and country, rustic folk of furthest lands,

DOER   plain people even, like ourselves,

SIDEMAN   sweet delight do

DOER   Sea of Ōmi

    AGEUTA
    on-w

CHORUS   ripples o! Sands of the shore may reach an end sands of the shore may reach an end; words of song, though, never shall. Greenwillow fronds flow on

always,   pine needles   do not fall and die.
Know then that the seed's the heart!   And though
times change,   though all things pass,   so long
as words   of these songs last,   so long shall
the bird prints run   so long shall   the bird
prints run.

MONDO
off-w*

SIDEMAN   <u>sp</u> Thank you. The old poets have left us many words,
but songs by women are rare. There are few like you,
old lady! 'My own love   this night shall come:
little spider   with her web   weaves me a sign!'
Is that a woman's song?

DOER   That's a song by Princess Sotōri, of the old days.
She was the consort of Emperor Ingyō. In form, at
least, it's her style I followed.

SIDEMAN   Well now, you say you followed Princess Sotōri's style?
Ono no Komachi herself, who's so much heard of in
recent years,

                    (Doer lowers her head.)

is said to work in Princess Sotōri's style. 'So
forlorn I grieve,   pondweed root-cut and drifting;
should some stream   stir to woo me now   I'd go,
I know!' There's a song by Komachi!

DOER   (lifting head)   <u>s</u> Yes, Ōe no Koreaki had had a
change of heart, and I was very downcast. <u>sp</u> Then
Fun'ya no Yasuhide, on his way down as Governor of
Mikawa, suggested I come with him. 'Do please find
solace in my country dwelling,' said he, [turning
to Sideman] and that was why I made the song.

SAGEUTA
on-w

           (turning front again) I'd forgotten   through the
years,   but listening now,   tears fall for old

        things   brought to mind   alas, with sorrow!

                (Doer checks tears.)

MONDO
off-w*

SIDEMAN $\underline{sp}$ How strange! I hear you say that it's you who
made the song, 'So forlorn I grieve' and your state-
ment that you followed Princess Sotōri's style
sounds like Komachi too. In fact, as I consider the
age . . . You, old lady, say you're a hundred; then
even if Komachi were much changed, she might well
still be alive. No, there's no longer any doubt:
you yourself are what is left of Komachi! $\underline{s}$ I
tell you, hide it no longer!

DOER   No, hearing 'Komachi'   I'm ashamed

           (She lifts her head, turns to Sideman.)

   'Hues all unseen . . .'   though then I sang,

AGEUTA
on-w

CHORUS   '. . . it shifts and fades,   a worldly one's
heart flower . . .' ah, now seen! I'm ashamed!

         (She lowers her head, turns front again.)

   ⁺So forlorn I grieve,   pondweed root-cut and drifting; should some stream   stir to woo me: even now
I'd go, I know!'   I'm ashamed!

         (Doer lifts her head once more. Sideman
and Child go back to sit at Sideman's spot.)

KURI
off-weak

   Indeed,   'screen them I do,   yet from these sleeves
spill shining drops,   of eyes that see thee not
the tears,' reigning   memories sow seeds   of passion
grasses'   bloom now wilted   I, until the end,   shall
hold--but why?--   with shining dews   to days long
since gone.

SASHI
off-weak

DOER   Yes, 'Absorbed in love   I lie me down   and he appears!'

CHORUS   sang I, though now   it suits me ill;   so long they've come,   the moons and years   I send off, greet,   as spring and fall   with dews trip in   and pass with frost,   for leaves of grass change, insect cries   have died away.

DOER   Already life   is at its term,

KUSE
on-weak

CHORUS   just like the rose of Sharon's   one glorious day. 'The living die,   the dead gain ever more   in this my life   alas, how long   am I bound to mourn?' That too I sang,   oh how long   the ivy vine, flowers falling,   leaves all dropping,   lingers in dewdrop life!

                (She lowers her head, lost in memories.)

Oh the old days,   I miss them so!   Each time I feel   one with the past   I so recall,   old things capture me,   till now, again,

                (She lifts her head, checks tears.)

I am in love   with those first years   of old age. Most piteous my plight!   In the old days   the very room   I lodged in   a single night   was decked with tortoiseshell;   the fence hung with   golden blossoms;   doorways dripped rock crystal;   Imperial Car,   court carriages   in radiant silks   of proudest hues   smooth-spread   pillows enhanced   the lovers' chamber   where, within,   I took my ease on flower-brocaded cushions.

                (She lowers her head.)

Now, a mud-daub hut's   my jeweled couch!

> (She lifts her head, listens to bell.)

DOER   Gateway Temple's   bell tolls

CHORUS   'All things must pass';   these old ears hear
             but learn nothing.   Winds sweep down

> (She looks into distance to her right.)

Osaka Pass: 'All born must die,'   they say;   oh,
if I knew!   When petals fly   and leaves fall, then,
each time,   for my delight,   here at my wattled
door

> (She takes one of the poem slips in her
> left hand, then uses fan to mime dipping a writing
> brush in ink. She writes, dips brush again, writes
> some more as Chorus sings on.)

the inkstone I make sing,   stain the brush, and
salt sea tangle   trace out leaves of speech   soon
withered quite.

> (She gazes at the slip she has been writing
> on.)

'Most affecting, but not strong.'   Not strong because
a woman's songs . . .

> (Weakly puts the poem slip down, and checks
> tears.)

So terribly   in my old age   I've grown weak,
till all that's left   is sorrow.

MONDO
off-sp

SIDEMAN   (to Sideman's Second)   You know, it's getting late
             for the feast of Seventh Night. Do invite the old
             lady to come along with us.

SIDE SECOND By all means.

> (Sideman's Second stands and moves a few
> steps toward Doer.)

I beg your pardon, old lady, but what harm could it do? Do please come and have a look at the celebration we're offering for Seventh Night.

DOER   Oh no, an old woman shouldn't impose that way. I wouldn't think of it.

                (Sideman's Second goes back to his place and sits. Sideman stands.)

SIDEMAN   No, no, old lady, we'll be glad to have you.

                (He goes up to Doer and touches her. She picks up her staff.)

Don't worry! Just come with us!

                (Doer stands, aided by Sideman, and emerges from the hut. At 'Komachi,' she goes to main spot while Sideman retires to Sideman's spot.)

AGEUTA
on-w

CHORUS   Seventh Night: weave streamer wands   to offer up how many years   gone shadow sere   Ono no Komachi's touched   one hundred,   overhead   Heaven's own congress of stars   with cloud walkers   quite at ease

                (Now Doer gazes at her sleeves. At 'poor woman,' she sits wearily, leaning on her staff, and lowers her head.)

did she brush sleeves,   now hempen-clad,   poor woman!   Oh painful fate!   A sight not to be borne!

                (Sideman opens his fan, holds it like a sake ladle, and faces Child. As Chorus sings on, Child opens his fan and holds it like a cup. He receives the liquor from Sideman, then goes before Doer and pours for her. At 'streamer wands,' he stands and begins to dance: at 'round cups go,' moves to mark post, then sweeps left up to drums; at 'oh lovely,' comes to center, opens.)

UTA
on-w

Ah yes, this night   for Seventh Night   ah yes, this night   for Seventh Night   offerings we have diverse,　some,　streamer wands　　twirling round

and round cups go　　while moon snow lights　　on

dancing children's sleeves,　　oh lovely scene!

EI
off-w

Fine bamboo wands　　with which we feast the Stars

DOER　　　　age to age jointed　　live on, headed hence

   (Child returns to Sideman's spot, does a
leftright, and sits.　Doer, as though unconsciously,
beats time with fan.)

CHORUS　　　to what eternities,　　Ten Thousand Years!

*
off-w*

DOER　　　　<u>sp</u> Oh, lovely　　they were just now,　　the dancing

children's sleeves!　　Long ago　　at Harvest Vigil

the girls of the Five Measure Dance　　twirled their

sleeves　　yes, five times it was; <u>s</u> sleeves offered

now　　for Seventh Night　　should be turned seven

times. <u>sp</u> When a madman runs, they say, the sane run

after him.　Now, lured by the dancing children's

sleeves, <u>s</u> the madman's going to run.

   (With the aid of her staff she stands,
then taps beat once.)

WAKA
off-w

One hundred years

MAI　　　　　 (She begins to dance, very slowly.　Some
way into the dance she lays down her staff, to
pick it up again near the end.　She stops at last
at main spot and, as text resumes, strikes fan
high pose.)

WAKA
off-w

One hundred years　　snug in a flower　　now dances

the butterfly.

   (Now she continues dancing, staff in hand.
At 'touching sight,' she does a leftright; at
'skirts,' moves to mark post; at 'wandering,' displays

open fan; at 'scarves,' turns left up to center;
at 'sleeves,' looks at sleeves.)

NORIJI
onori-w

CHORUS   Oh touching sight!   Oh touching sight!   The old
tree bough   blossoms

DOER   nod, swinging sleeves   move how forgotten

CHORUS   skirts keep feeble step,

DOER   a wandering wave's

CHORUS   up and dancing   scarves toss round   but no sleeves
these   to turn back the old days!

DOER   <u>off</u> Oh the past, I miss it so!

(She sits at center, staff held over left
shoulder, and hides tears. At 'all the while,'
she lifts her head; then gazes up to the eastern
sky; then listens to temple bell and to cockcrow;
at 'caught me,' lowers head.)

NORIJI
onori-w

CHORUS   All the while   the short night   of early fall
begins to break,   Gateway Temple's bell,

DOER   cocks a-crowing

CHORUS   tell abroad dawn's   caught me, ah,

DOER   the Forest of Vergogne

(She stands, leaning on her staff.)

never will hide me now.

(She bows her head toward Sideman, then
makes her way toward hut.)

Farewell,   I'm going back,   says she,   leans on
her staff   and totters home   to the straw hut
whence she came;

(She enters hut and sits facing front, with
staff over her right shoulder.)

a hundred-year-old crone   is she called now,   the
ruin of Komachi

        (She checks tears.)

is she called now,   the ruin of Komachi.

        (While music is still playing, she comes
    out of hut and stands motionless.)

GARGOYLE
(Oni-gawara)

(Lord and Tarōkaja enter. Tarōkaja sits
at back of stage, while Lord comes down front.)

LORD I'm a great lord, famous to the furthest corners of
the land. After a long period of residence in Miyako,
I find that my lawsuit has gone wholly in my favor.
I've been granted letters patent confirming me in my
fief, and indeed have seen my lands most graciously
and most generously increased. What's more, I've even
received leave to go home. Never has there been such
good fortune. I'll call Tarōkaja right away, and
make him happy too. (He goes toward flute post.)
Ahoy! Ahoy! Tarōkaja! You out there?

TARŌKAJA (stands) YESSIR!

LORD You there? You there? (He goes to Sideman's spot.)

TARŌKAJA (proceeding to main spot) YESSIR!

LORD You're here?

TARŌKAJA (dropping to one knee) I'm right here, sir!

LORD Good lord, you're fast. But stand up.

TARŌKAJA (standing) Very good, sir.

LORD There's no panic, you know. After a long period of
residence in Miyako, I find my lawsuit has gone exactly
as I wished. I've been granted letters patent confirming me in my fief, and in fact I've seen my lands
most graciously and most generously increased. If
that isn't good fortune, what is?

TARŌKAJA You've been looking forward to this for ages, sir,
and now it's worked out. It's just wonderful.

LORD Right! Right! And now I think of it, I've something
else to make you happy.

TARŌKAJA	Why, sir, what could it be?
LORD	I've got leave to go home!
TARŌKAJA	Better and better, sir. All your dreams are coming true.
LORD	My very thought. But you know, the reason everything's gone exactly as I wished must be the blessing of that Yakushi I always pray to at Inaba Hall. I'd like to go thank him and say good-bye, because once I'm home I won't be able to worship there any more. What do you think?
TARŌKAJA	A marvelous idea, sir.
LORD	Then let's go. You too.
TARŌKAJA	By all means, sir.
LORD	(begins walking around stage) Now, now, come, come.
TARŌKAJA	(following behind) I'm coming, sir, I'm coming.
LORD	My, my, at home they don't know a thing about all this, they're on pins and needles watching for me to be back any moment.
TARŌKAJA	As you say, sir, they're on pins and needles expecting you back from one instant to the next.
LORD	When I get there and tell them my good fortune, I'm sure they'll be delighted.
TARŌKAJA	Thoroughly delighted, sir.
LORD	(stopping at center) Heavens! Hardly two words we've said to each other, and here we are already in the blessed presence.
TARŌKAJA	We are indeed, sir.
LORD	You come on over and pray too.
TARŌKAJA	Very good, sir.

                          (They sit side by side down front. Each
                          lays his open fan before him, and with an exaggerated
                          gesture joins his palms in an attitude of prayer.)

LORD   You know, it's so wonderfully peaceful every time you
                  come here, isn't it!

TAROKAJA   It really is, sir. Perfectly peaceful.

LORD   You know what I'm thinking? I'm thinking that it's
                  this blessed Yakushi I have to thank for everything:
                  all my good fortune, my being able to go home . . .
                  So when I get there, I'm going to build him a chapel.
                  What do you say?

TAROKAJA   A marvelous idea, sir.

LORD   Then I'd like to model it after this Hall here, the
                  place being so beautiful and all; though of course I
                  couldn't make mine nearly as fine. So, Tarokaja, let's
                  you and I both have a good look around, and take note
                  of everything.

TAROKAJA   I'm with you, sir!

                          (They stand and peer at the Hall.)

LORD   Bless my soul, what an elegant Hall it is!

TAROKAJA   It is, sir.

LORD   That carving, for instance, on the lattice over the
                  door. Whew! That's fine workmanship!

TAROKAJA   Fine, sir, for certain.

LORD   As long as we're at it, let's go look at the place
                  from the rear.

TAROKAJA   A good idea, sir.

LORD   (walking)   Now, now, come, come.

TAROKAJA   (following behind)   I'm coming, sir, I'm coming!

LORD   It's real Hida carpenters built this Hall, they say.
                  Handsome from absolutely every angle, isn't it!

TAROKAJA   Truly, sir, from every angle a handsome Hall.

                    (By this time, Lord is at Sideman's spot.
                    He now goes up to main spot, then back to Sideman's
                    spot, gawking the while.)

LORD   Uhuh . . . Arc beams, froglegs, windbreak . . .
            Heavens! Tarokaja!

TAROKAJA   (at main spot)   What, sir?

LORD   What's that on top of that windbreak?

TAROKAJA   Why, sir, don't you know?

LORD   No indeed.

TAROKAJA   That's a gargoyle, sir.

LORD   A gargoyle?

TAROKAJA   Yes, sir.

LORD   Oof, gargoyles are pretty scary things, arne't they!

TAROKAJA   Yes, sir.

LORD   Take a good look at that gargoyle. Doesn't it remind
            you of someone?

TAROKAJA   No, sir. How could anyone possibly look like that
            gargoyle?

LORD   No, no, it struck me that gargoyle's the spitting
            image of somebody or other. Can't get who it is,
            though. Ah! I've got it! I've got it!

                    (He bursts out crying.)

TAROKAJA   What's going on? Please, sir, what's making you
            carry on this way?

LORD   Well, you see, I was sure the gargoyle reminded me of
            somebody--and it's the spitting image of my wife back
            home!

                    (He cries some more.)

TAROKAJA	Now that you mention it, sir, it <u>does</u> look a lot like her.
LORD	Those popping eyes, and that hooked nose--isn't it her very portrait?
TAROKAJA	Definitely, sir, her very portrait.
LORD	And that mouth, gaping clean up to the earbones! Goodness, that's exactly the way she looks every time she bawls you out!
TAROKAJA	You're right, sir, that's exactly how Madam looks every time she bawls me out.
LORD	No one here can have laid eyes on my wife, and yet there she is! It's unbelievable!
TAROKAJA	Truly unbelievable, sir.
LORD	One look at that gargoyle and I'm so homesick for my wife I can't stand it!
TAROKAJA	I must say, sir, that I certainly don't blame you. (Lord cries some more.) But sir, do calm down a bit and listen to me. With all your good fortune, you have leave to head right home anyway. So you'll be seeing her in the flesh! There's nothing to cry about. You've really got to cheer up.
LORD	Hmm. You're absolutely right. If I head right home, I'll see her in the flesh. And anyway, with all my good fortune there's nothing to cry about. Let's cheer up and both go back roaring with laughter!
TAROKAJA	A fine idea, sir.
LORD	You go over there.
TAROKAJA	(moving off a little) As you wish, sir.
LORD	Further!
TAROKAJA	(complying) Very good, sir.

LORD   All the way!

TARŌKAJA   YESSIR! (He goes to mark post.)

LORD   Now, LAUGH!

                      (Both roar with laughter. Lord exits,
                followed by Tarōkaja.)

THE BOAT BRIDGE
(Funabashi: a fourth-category play)

The Boat Bridge is set in cherry blossom time, but the season
only heightens, by contrast, its grim mood. The subject is stark
tragedy. Long ago, a young man and a young girl who lived on opposite
sides of a river fell in love, and the man began crossing a pontoon
bridge to the girl every night. The parents of both disapproved,
however, and they pried loose the planks of the bridge so that both
lovers fell in and drowned. They sank into hell and were pinned with
boulders beneath the waters of the river of the underworld, where they
had to stand as bridge pilings.

No play could make clearer than this one does the essential
traits of an obsession play. The Boat Bridge, which is Zeami's revi-
sion of an older, anonymous work, is almost primitive in its rough
colors, its bony contours, and its concrete symbols. The breaking of
the bridge and the drownings are indeed a thorough way to picture
rupture of contact; the talk of boat bridge and anchored bridge con-
trasts lightness and heaviness; the crushing boulders and the ice of
hell show frozen, solitary agony; and the final floating up of the
bridge, now whole, and of the phantoms themselves, conveys sudden and
almost unbelievable salvation. Even the Man'yōshū poem which is the
seed of The Boat Bridge is exploited to suggest an unbridgeable gulf:
it contains the syllables to-ri-ha-na-shi which can actually mean
either 'break apart' or 'there is no bird.' The link established between these two apparently unrelated meanings is analogous itself to
a bridge.

The tale of The Boat Bridge is well known in Japan, for there
are many stories and plays about lovers separated by a river. The
lovers often take the form of a pair of mountains called imose-yama,
and the river which parts them is called imose-gawa, the 'lovers'
river.' The most famous such river is in the mountains of Yoshino,
far from northern Japan where the play takes place.

Though distant, Yoshino is not foreign to The Boat Bridge, for
that is probably where the Sideman comes from. The Sideman is actually
a yamabushi, a member of an ancient order that associates certain
Esoteric Buddhist practices with the power of sacred mountains. The
peaks above the village of Yoshino, some way south of Miyako on the Kii
Peninsula, are the most sacred of all. Connected with them are the
nearby massif of Kazuraki (nowadays pronounced Katsuragi) and the
Triple Shrine of Kumano, made up of two shrines and of the Nachi
waterfall.

The yamabushi order was founded about 700 A.D. by the semi-
legendary En the Upāsaka (En no Ubasoku, often known as En no Gyōja).
Upāsaka is a Sanskrit word that means a lay Buddhist devotee, and the
yamabushi have always been laymen. In pre-modern Japan they were the
local wise men and healers, and were often reputed to have magic
powers. En the Upāsaka himself is said to have made a magic rock
bridge from Kazuraki to Ōmine, the Great Peak above Yoshino. One of
his supernatural helpers, however, the female god of Kazuraki, was so
ashamed of her own ugliness that she would only work by night. Hence,
the bridge could not be made perfect. This god's name was Hitokoto-
nushi-no-mikoto, 'Mistress of the Single Word.'

The Boat Bridge contains two quotations from a scripture about
one of the main yamabushi deities, Fudō the Unmoving, though Fudō is
not actually named. The scripture says, 'Those who see my body conceive wisdom.' Though Fudō's body is in many respects the sacred
mountain itself, this is what he looks like in human form: he is
blue-black in color, and sits or stands on a rock with a raised sword
in his right hand and a coiled rope in his left. His face wears an
expression of ferocious energy, tusks protrude from his mouth, and he
is enveloped in fire. His mantram, translated, is, 'I dedicate myself
to the Universal Diamond; be this raging fury destroyed!' The fury is
not his, but the devotee's. It is the rage of which Yoshitsune speaks
in Yashima, the obsessive fury of wrongful clinging. For Fudō with his
sword cuts the bonds of clinging, and with his rope binds the twin
demons of birth-and-death.

SHIDAI

> (Sideman and Sideman's Second enter, and
> stand facing each other down front.)

SHIDAI
on-str

SIDEMAN AND
SIDE SECOND

Mountain past mountain   lies the goal   mountain
past mountain   lies the goal,   its cloud trails
shall guide our way.

> (Sideman faces front.)

NANORI
off-sp

SIDEMAN

I'm a roving monk just come from the Triple Shrine
of Kumano. As I've never seen Matsushima or Hirai-
zumi, I've made up my mind to hurry there this very
spring.

> (They face each other again.)

AGEUTA
on-str

SIDEMAN AND
SIDE SECOND

All shallow fords   runs Yasu River   all shallow
fords   runs Yasu River;   Seventh Night's   promised
union,   one night a year,   is a vain dream   soon
Broken Well's   posthouse is past,

> (Sideman takes few steps to show travel.
> By the end of this passage he returns to his place,
> and faces front.)

a chill wind   down Mount Ibuki   cries alone   as
haze veils the moon,   and now we pass   from Mino to
Owari;   life's sure end   then ponder, old age,
the warning comes   then ponder, old age,   the warning
comes.

TSUKI-
ZERIFU
off-sp

SIDEMAN

Hurrying so, here we are already at a place called
Sano, in the land of Kōzuke. I'll ask for shelter
nearby.

| | (Sideman and Sideman's Second retire to Sideman's spot. Second enters, followed by Doer. |
| ISSEI | Second, wearing <u>tsure</u> mask, stands at center; Doer, who wears no mask, stands at main spot. They face each other.) |

ISSEI
off-str

DOER, SECOND   It's to the Law   we'll build a way   across a boat bridge,   our fond hope   for the life beyond.

(Doer faces front.)

SASHI
off-str

DOER   'Vast are days now gone,'   and all things   behind us stretch   a floating bridge of dreams;

(They face each other.)

DOER, SECOND   there boats throng,   contending,   on the river Hori Inlet's   banks give no safe haven,   empty waves   back to the sad world   roll the Six Ways, none evade them.

SAGEUTA
on-str

A burning love   from the old days,   down the past's far reaches,   draws my heart,

AGEUTA
on-str

and lives gone by   whose reward   is this birth now   whose reward   is this birth now   so fill my mind   that for me,   there is no way   across the sea   of birth-and-death   a bridge of boats I'll build!   The twin streams run

(Doer moves to center, Second to mark post.)

with one bright way between,   while sins propose paths by the score.   It's a true bridge   I'd lay across   it's a true bridge   I'd lay across!

MONDO
off

DOER   <u>sp</u> Come, you roving monk, give to our bridge-
building fund before you pass!

SIDEMAN   You're laymen, I see. Why, it's wonderful that you
actually mean to build a bridge here!

DOER   I'm surprised at you, making remarks like that. Our
not being religious, you know, doesn't at all mean
that there's nothing to us. Just make your contribution before you go.

SIDEMAN   Certainly I'll make a contribution. But when was it
that a boat bridge was first thrown across here?

DOER   Don't you grasp the meaning of the <u>Man'yōshū</u> poem
that says, 'At Sano   on the Eastland Way   the boat
bridge   lies broken now . . .'?

SECOND   <u>w</u> No, when you talk that way, I'm ashamed! Dismal
our past, when

DOER   <u>str</u> passion-driven,   we sank in this stream:

           (Doer and Second face each other.)

DOER, SECOND   and therefore   we must talk less. Still, across
Three Shallows River   and all its pain,   lay, we
pray you,   a bridge of boats

           (They press toward Sideman.)

that buoyant we may walk!

KAKEAI
off

SIDEMAN   <u>sp</u> Ah yes, I recognize the story about the lovers
whom their parents parted. <u>str</u> So, you're helping
those who of old   made the boat bridge--   am I
right?

DOER   <u>sp</u> Especially you,   a yamabushi   must help us
to build the bridge.

SIDEMAN <u>str</u> So just because   I'm a yamabushi,   I myself
must build you your bridge?

DOER <u>sp</u> Don't argue so.   En the Upāsaka,   in Kazuraki,
prayed a bridge into being   on the Kume road: so,
what do you say?

SECOND <u>w</u> Not that I compare,   but she too   is a woman,
the goddess   of Kazuraki,   She of the Single Word;

DOER <u>sp</u> nor is it   with one word only   we'll keep you
here,   but time and again: this rock bridge,

SECOND <u>w</u> why in your heart   will you not lay it down?

(They face each other.)

DOER, SECOND <u>str</u> Nonetheless,   I do hear tell   that in Kazuraki
the rock bridge   was made by night,   <u>w</u> so that in
fact

(They press toward Sideman.)

it could hardly   have reached the other side.

(They face front.)

UTA
on-w

CHORUS Long this spring day,   the water calm: a bridge
of boats

(Doer advances a little, opens.)

will need no pilings,   o yamabushi,   it's wastefully
these ruins decay:

(They turn to Sideman.)

please lay the bridge!

(Doer turns front again; Second goes to
sit before Chorus.)

AGEUTA
on-w

Here we are then   at Sano crossing   here we are
then   at Sano crossing,   in dim twilight:

(Doer comes down front and faces Sideman.)

will you brush your sleeves clean   and pass on by?

       (He moves to mark post, then turns left
toward main spot.)

Spring is the season,   the river breeze   blows
blossoms over;   now, a road   for the Law to
travel,   a boat bridge,

       (On the way to main spot, Doer turns to
Sideman.)

oh lay for us,   you yamabushi!   From peak to peak
you make your rounds,   yet if you crossed no streams,

       (At main spot, he turns again to Sideman.)

where could you go?

*
off-sp

SIDEMAN

Now, the poem in the <u>Man'yōshū</u> can be read to mean
either, 'At Sano   on the Eastland Way   the boat
bridge   lies broken now . . .' or, 'At Sano   on
the Eastland Way,   a boat bridge,   and there's no
bird . . .' Why is this?

DOER

Well, there is indeed a story about that. I'll tell
it to you.

       (He sits at center.)

KATARI
off-w*

<u>sp</u> A man who lived here long ago had a secret love in
a place across the river; so nightly he crossed the
boat bridge to her. The parents on both sides were
greatly displeased, and they broke loose the planks
of the bridge. When he, all unsuspecting, set foot
on the bridge he so dearly trusted, he fell into the
water and died. <u>s</u> Whether it was   wrongful clinging
or his karma,   straight he sank   into the River of

Three Fords,   froze in the ice   of the Great Scarlet
Lotus Hell,

UTA
on-w

CHORUS   to rise no more,   for such a sea of pain   there is
                   indeed,   and there, under the bridge,   by boulders
                   crushed,   knew tortue.

KUSE
on-w

                   But his sinking   stopped not there,   for the soul
                   too   racked the body,   he in his heart turned
                   fiend.   Passion grasses   still grew lush,   lustful
                   desires   burned on in him . . .   Old the bridge,
                   old the story,   and I the one   whose tale it tells.
                   I beg,   comfort my shade!

DOER   The evening sun   at last sinks low,

                          (Doer looks up at sky toward his right.
                   At 'rain,' he stands and advances a little toward
                   front; at 'vanishes,' goes to mark post, then
                   sweeps left up to drums, then moves to center; at
                   'bell,' turns right and up to main spot, intently
                   listening; at first 'he is gone,' opens toward
                   front.)

CHORUS   the misted sky   grows dark;   clouds form, and rain--
                   the bardo now comes near,   for what seemed bridge
                   vanishes;   here indeed,   'at Sano   on the Eastland
                   Way   the boat bridge   lies broken now,'   and a bell
                   tolls: twilight turns   the sky to night,   and he
                   is gone   the sky to night,   and he is gone.

                          (Doer exits. Second withdraws to stagehand
                   spot. The Fool, who some time ago slipped in to
MONDO &   sit at Fool's spot, now stands. He ends up, by the
KATARI   usual sort of process, sitting at center, where he
                   repeats to Sideman the story of the bridge. He adds,
                   however, the following.)

FOOL   . . . Then the girl got so worried that her lover
                   hadn't come--he was very faithful, you see--that she
                   started across the bridge herself, fell in, and drowned

too. The parents of both of them searched for the
bodies, and since they'd heard that a cock would crow
over a sunken corpse, they went looking for a cock.
But there turned out not to be a single cock in all of
Sano. That's why the poem can be read either as
'lies broken now,' or as 'there's no bird.'

> (After a suitable exchange of politenesses
> with Sideman, Fool returns to Fool's spot. He will
> slip out after Doer's entrance.)

AGEUTA
on-str

SIDEMAN AND   The ruins, grown old now,   shall we change   the
SIDE SECOND   ruins, grown old now,   shall we change,   and by the
grace   of the Three Treasures   wipe out all sins
of the Five Ways;   for very great   is the power of
the Law   for very great   is the power of the Law.

DEHA   (Doer enters, now wearing the awa-otoko
mask, and with a demon mallet slung across his
back. He stands at first pine, facing front.
Second stands, and comes to main spot; she faces
Sideman.)

SASHI
off-str

SECOND   Oh roving monk,   I thank you!   Wantonly did I sink
in the Three Fords,   yet now believe   that by Dharma-
might   the bridge of boats   floats, and I, o
precious gift,   rise again!

> (Doer turns to Sideman.)

DOER   Oh roving monk!   Not yet can I,   by wrongful clinging   held fast, float   free of the bridge   piling
on me   heavy agonies

> (He presses toward Sideman.)

I'll show you now.

KAMI-
NO-EI
off-str

'The tears I weep,

>   (He looks up at sky to his right, then
>   stamps several beats.)

oh, would they fall as rain!   For should that River
rise,   that you've to cross,

ISSEI
off-str

you might come back!'

>   (He opens toward front.)

CHORUS   Come back, oh, come back!   Oh empty wave

>   (He points at his own head with fan.)

DOER   washed pilings weight my head,   boulders pin me,
crushed, in agony.

>   (Second goes before drums, as Doer moves
>   to main spot.)

CHORUS   See now, see!   A ghastly vision!

>   (Doer stamps several beats, then goes to
>   mark post.)

SASHI
off-str

DOER   'Those who see my body, conceive wisdom':

>   (He sweeps his gaze around, down low, then
>   turns left up to main spot; there, he opens, and
>   salutes Sideman with joined palms.)

this power   I do now receive.   Where once I was
dust at the bottom   of Hell's gulf,   'Those who
know my mind, in this flesh grow to Buddhahood';
ah, the precious gift!

KAKEAI
off

SIDEMAN   <u>str</u> Oh painful sight!   Lustful karma   still runs

deep: shake off this clinging   and go on,   lament,
lament the past!

SECOND   Yes, by lamenting,   everything,   all clouds of sin,
will melt away,   and True Semblance,   the moon,
rise at last.

DOER   The Five Blocks' mist   shall hardly clear   this spring
night: a moment now,   as in dream   sports a butterfly,   come, I'll show you   the scene itself.

> (Second goes to Sideman's spot and sits
> Sideman and Sideman's Second move aside a little
> to make room for her.)

SECOND   <u>w</u> No Yoshino   is this place,   yet here too runs   a
Lovers' River;

DOER   <u>sp</u> the bridge was cut,   but little I knew,   who each
night

SECOND   <u>str</u> crossed eagerly   the bridge of boats,

DOER   ardent in love

> (Doer presses toward Second.)

for my dearest.

TACHI-
MAWARI

> (Doer moves quietly to mark post, then turns
> left up to drums. No particular meaning is ascribed
> to this <u>tachimawari</u>. As text resumes, he faces
> front from main spot.)

WAKA
off-str

Yes, nightly,   a well-known way   I follow   over the
bridge

> (He looks up to his right at sky.)

NORIJI
onori-str

arches the clear sky   bright with a moon   now halfway
to rest,

CHORUS   and people too   lie all asleep;

                          (He goes toward Bridgeway.)

                at the third quarter of the Ox,   cold the air,
                the river wind   that I like well,

                          (At first pine, he gazes into distance
                     toward front.)

                far yonder where we meet,   on the far bank,   I
                see someone: oh, is it she?

                          (He strikes excitement pose.)

                Oh happiness!   She is faithful!

                          (Now he stumps several beats. At second
                     'between,' he comes foward a little, strikes cloud
                     fan pose and gazes as though at far bank; at 'mag-
                     pies,' comes in to main spot; at 'nearly joined,'
                     moves down front and stamps beat; at 'dropped,'
                     drops dramatically to a sitting position, lowers
                     head.)

NORIJI
onori-str

                So each spied each,   while between   so each spied

                each,   while between   stretched the bridge;   and

                on we came   as waves rush to meet,   as magpies

                gather, linking wings   into a bridge,   and nearly

                joined: when loosened planks   gave way underfoot:

                in we dropped suddenly,   and sank.

                          (Now he lifts head, chants boldly.)

KAMI-
NO-EI
off-str

DOER   'At Sano   on the Eastland Way   the boat bridge

                lies broken now,   by parents parted: I'll see my

                love no more.'

                          (Below, at second 'we turned,' slips fan
                     into sash, takes hold of demon mallet; at 'were
                     stood,' holds mallet vertical before his chest,
                     with both hands; at 'serpent,' stands, goes to

> mark post, then turns left and up to flute; at
> 'lustful,' moves to center, brandishes mallet,
> stamps several beats; then goes down on one
> knee, pivots to face front; then glares at Sideman;
> at first 'bright bridge,' stands, goes to mark
> post; at second 'bright bridge,' moves to main
> spot; at first 'on high,' opens toward front and
> joins palms.)

CHU-
NORIJI
on-w

Then we turned   to fiends of clinging

CHORUS

then we turned   to fiends of clinging,   and there,

side by side, were stood   in the River of Three

Fords,   as bridge pilings.   Our aspect changed

to foul serpent;   soon enough   did wrongful cling-

ing   to our world,   to birth-and-death,   make

of us   lustful demons.   So we were racked,   and

sank in pain.   Yet, roving monk,   by your power,

by your Dharma-savor,   the bright bridge   of truth

illumined   the bright bridge   of truth illumined,

on high rising now,   I float at last   on high rising

now,   I float at last.

(Facing side, Doer stamps final beat.)

LAYMAN SELFSAME
(Jinen koji: a miscellaneous play)

Layman Selfsame says nothing about the season, nor is it ghastly, poetic, or sublime. Instead, it is a thriller with some song and dance worked in. The role of the Layman is a real showpiece for an actor, and originally that actor was Kannami. Kannami wrote the play, and loved to perform it.

Nowadays actors give the Layman an air of dignified maturity, but Kannami played him as a youth of about sixteen. Whether or not there ever was a real Layman Selfsame—one document says he was the disciple of a certain thirteenth-century Zen master—Kannami's Layman Selfsame is not nearly as far from the Lady of Mouth-of-Sound as one might think. He is indeed a character who appears all through Japanese theater: the handsome, irresistibly charming youth who turns out to be the perfectly gallant lover, the ultimate sword fighter, or . . . a Bodhisattva. Not that Layman Selfsame is an announced Bodhisattva, however. He has no time for fancy titles. He is much too busy working (with incomparable nonchalance and effectiveness) for the good, and succoring maidens in distress.

The Layman's name in Japanese is Jinen; this is the same word that, read shizen, means 'nature' in the modern language. His title, koji, refers to a kind of lay monk who had not taken formal vows or shaved his head. Jinen Koji, in other words, means Mr. Natural, Mr. Himself, Mr. Just-As-He-Is. He is always precisely the same as himself, and equal to all things.

It is delightful to compare Layman Selfsame with such plays as

Komachi on the Gravepost or Granny Mountains, which announce the deep
truth that good and evil are one. For the Layman says, 'When it comes
to understanding good and evil, the girl is good and the traders are
evil, and both paths, good and evil, are as plain as plain can be
right here.' Good and evil may be one, but in action, right is not
the same as wrong, or down as up.

As Layman Selfsame is a hero of the Dharma, one should know what
the Dharma is. The basic meaning of this Sanskrit word is 'law,' but
in Buddhism a dharma is first of all a thing or event. All dharmas,
or things, change from and into something else. No dharma has unvary-
ing, permanent existence, and anything one can taste, touch, smell,
see, hear, or name (for consciousness is one of the six senses) is a
dharma. A dharma is not unreal, but it is provisional. It is a form-
in-transformation, like a wave. Any wave on the sea is water. Thus
the Heart of Wisdom Sutra says, 'Form (dharma, wave) is nothingness
(the eternally real, water) and nothingness is form.'

Hence this 'nothingness' is also dharma, in this sense usually
written Dharma. As 'law,' Dharma means 'the way things are,' 'the
way it is.' The Dharma-body of the Buddha is everything, yet no
particular thing; it is the way all things, or dharmas, truly are.
But since emptiness is also form, Dharma also means Wave: the Teaching
and practice of the Buddha. Sometimes this teaching takes such human
form as that of Layman Selfsame, of the Lady of Mouth-of-Sound, or of
the historical Buddha. In truth, though, the voice of the Dharma-body
comes from all things. All things are, and manifest, Dharma equally.
Therefore, not only is 'each sound of beings feeling and non-feeling'

a song, but it is really, though infinitely diverse, the same song:
the voice of the Dharma.

There is an old saying, found at least in some Japanese Zen
writings, that singing and dancing are the voice of the Dharma. No
doubt that is why the Layman has been known to dance on the preacher's
high seat, and no doubt that is why Kannami himself, and Zeami, can
pass on so much without seeming to, from the stage. Their way is
what the Layman calls 'Playful Words and Gorgeous Language.' "Gorgeous Language,' kigyo, is one of the ten sins any Buddhist is en-
joined not to commit. And yet, because 'Back links it is that lift
one high,' and others high as well, the Bodhisattva, to lead beings
on toward illumination, may well use the highly attractive devices of
art.

Thus Layman Selfsame does after all have his subtleties. He is
remarkable, in fact, for being as much Sideman as Doer, for his role
is analogous to that of the husband in The Block. (The slave trader,
whose profession flourished in medieval Japan, is a purely technical
Sideman.) He is deeply involved, but he is a spectator at the same
time. As his steadfast attentiveness saves the girl only in the
furthest place, at the last moment, the play is a regular fourth-
position play after all.

(Fool enters and stops at main spot.)

NANORI
off-sp

FOOL   I'm a fellow who lives near Cloud Lodge Temple in the
        Eastern Hills. There's an acolyte here, called Lay-
        man Selfsame, who's preaching the Dharma a whole
        seven days. Today's the day his vow will be met.
        Everyone! Gather round and lend an ear!

                (He goes to start of bridgeway, facing
                curtain. After next line he kneels on one knee
                at stagehand spot, back to stage.)

*
off-sp

        Tell him to please come right away!

                (Doer enters, wearing kasshiki mask. He
                faces front from bridgeway, and addresses an
                imagined throng.)

*
off-sp

DOER   Request pledge cards, if you please, for the rebuild-
        ing of Cloud Lodge Temple!

                (He goes to center and sits there on a
                stool provided by Fool. Fool then sits at Fool's
                spot.)

*
off-str*

DOER $\underline{sp}$ Evening brings rain   cloud lodge temple,
        waiting for the moon   I'll pass the time with a
        turn at   preaching Dharma,   says he,   mounts the
        Master's High Seat,   rings the Dedication Bell:
        (joining palms) $\underline{s}$ In reverence and awe I declare:
        to the Lifelong Master Teacher, Shakyamuni of the
        Precious Name, to the Buddhas of the Three Ages, to
        the Bodhisattvas of the Ten Directions, humbly I
        speak, and to all protecting powers offer the Heart
        of Wisdom Sutra.

>   (During above passage, Child enters and
>   starts down bridgeway. She has a robe over her
>   arm and carries a letter. Seeing her, Fool
>   mutters, 'Oh, the poor thing!' and takes robe
>   and letter from her, then sits her down near mark
>   post. Fool then spreads robe on the ground before
>   Doer and, dropping to one knee, offers Doer the
>   letter.)

MONDO
off-sp

DOER   Ah, is this a prayer petition you're giving me?

FOOL   Well, there's a beautiful robe here. Do please hurry
              up and read the prayer petition.

>   (Doer takes the letter. Fool returns to
>   Fool's spot, while Doer opens letter and holds it
>   reverently lifted with both hands.)

*
off-str*

DOER   <u>sp</u> 'Reverently I declare: concerning a request for

              prayers to comfort the departed. Herewith, one offer-

              ing for the Three Treasures and for all monks. To

              wit, from my earnest desire that the souls of my two

              parents instantly know the Buddha-fruit, I humbly

              donate to the Three Treasures <u>s</u> one humble shroud.'

>   (He lowers letter, visibly moved.)

              The Indian pauper woman   offered a garment to the

              monks   to assure her own future life;   but now a

              pauper girl   for her parents . . .

>   (He lifts letter again and goes on reading.)

AGEUTA
on-w

CHORUS   'One humble shroud   so costly   one humble shroud

              so costly,   this sorry life   I'd quickly leave

              and with dear father,   with dear mother,   come to

              birth   on one same lotus throne.'

>   (He touches the letter to his forehead,
>   then hides tears.)

So to all reads   Layman Selfsame,   wetting his
ink-black sleeves,   till the whole throng,   one
by one,   leaves no sleeve   unwet with tears   leaves
no sleeve   unwet with tears.

> (During above passage, Sideman and
> Sideman's Second enter. Sideman stands at first
> pine, facing front, while Sideman's Second kneels
> on one knee at second pine.)

NANORI
off-sp

SIDEMAN   You have before you a slave merchant from the lands
to the east. I've just been up to Miyako, where I
purchased many persons. Among them, I bought a girl
of no more than thirteen or fourteen. Yesterday, she
begged leave to go away for a while, so I allowed
her to do so. However, she isn't back yet.

> (He turns to Sideman's Second.)

MONDO
off-sp

Hey, are you there? That young girl we had yesterday
said something about memorial prayers for her parents,
so I suppose she must be attending the preaching.
Layman Selfsame's at Cloud Lodge Temple, so let's go
have a look.

SIDE SECOND   That's fine with me.

> (They start toward stage. Sideman imme-
> diately spots Child.)

MONDO
off-sp

SIDEMAN   I knew it! There she is! You go bring her here.

> (He motions to Sideman's Second, who goes
> up to Child.)

SIDE SECOND   Get up!

> (He leads her toward Sideman's spot.
> Startled, Fool stands and heads for first pine.)

FOOL   You won't get away with this!

                    (Sideman turns to Fool and brandishes a sword.)

SIDEMAN   I've business with her.

FOOL   Oh well, if you've business with her, go ahead.

                    (Sideman walks cooly past Doer to Sideman's spot. Sideman, Sideman's Second, and Child all sit in a line. Fool rushes down to mark post and drops to one knee facing Doer.)

MONDO
off-sp

DOER   What is it?

FOOL   Well, sir, it's the girl who gave you the prayer petition just now. Two toughs came and took her away with them. I told them they wouldn't get away with it. But they said they had business with her, so I let them go.

DOER   Ah, this is terrible! From the start there was something striking about that girl. And when she gave me the prayer petition, the way she wrote 'humble shroud' instead of just 'robe' did surprise me somewhat. As far as I can see, she traded her own person for that robe, so as to bring comfort to her parents, and then offered it up with her prayer petition. And in that case, the men just now must have been slave traders. Since they had their claim and we had none, you could hardly have stopped them.

FOOL   If they were slave traders, they must have gone down to the East. (jumping up) I'll run to Ōtsu-Matsumoto and stop them there!

DOER   Just a minute!

                    (Fool kneels on one knee again.)

You'd never be able to manage it. I myself will take

this robe, exchange it for the girl, and bring her back here.

FOOL   But that'll waste all the preaching you've done so far.

DOER   Oh no, people could hear me preach a hundred or a thousand days. But when it comes to understanding good and evil, the girl is good and the traders are evil, and both paths, good and evil, are as plain as plain can be right here. Do you see what I mean?

> (At approximately this point, Sideman and Sideman's Second turn their backs to the stage and, as though invisible, prepare for the next scene. They bare their right arm and shoulder, and each grasps a punting pole in his left hand. Then, as Doer concludes his preaching, Fool folds the robe into a long band and drapes it round Doer's neck from the rear. At 'at one,' Doer stands, holding the two ends of the robe in his left hand. The effect of the brilliantly patterned cloth against his somber garment is very striking. Fool removes stool and takes it to stagehand's spot, then exits. Doer proceeds, chanting, toward bridgeway.)

*
off-str

DOER   The preaching is over for today. (joining palms and bowing) I pray with this merit to touch all things, that beings and I at one grow to

ISSEI
off-str

the Buddha-way   I've to practice,

CHORUS   yes, renounce   the self did she   and I must save her.

> (Doer's progress signifies his journey to Lake Biwa, over the Osaka Pass. Now, Sideman and Sideman's Second stand and take their poles in both hands.)

ISSEI
off-str

SIDEMAN AND   Now outward   whither bound   with white waves breaking
SIDE SECOND   down the ship lanes   hurry, hurry on!

(Doer has arrived at third pine. He spots
Sideman, and steps quickly toward him while pointing with his fan.)

DOER   Boat I have none,   but in the way

CHORUS   of the Law I preach,   let your hearts rest,   and
stop!

MONDO
off-str*

DOER   <u>sp</u> Ahoy, the boat out there! I've got to talk to
you!

SIDEMAN   This isn't the ferry for Yamada or Yabase. What's
it you're calling us for?

DOER   (standing now at main spot)   I'm not a traveler,
either. I'm not calling any ferry. You're the boat
I want to talk to.

SIDEMAN   Do you? What kind of boat do you think this is?

DOER   A slave traders' boat. I want to talk to you.

SIDEMAN   No good, you're shouting too loud! What's that?
What's that?

DOER   Of course, of course, you're afraid other people will
hear; of course you feel I'm shouting too loud. I
didn't say 'slave traders,' I said 'stave traders.'
I was talking about the staves you have aboard.

SIDE SECOND   <u>s</u> Timber, yes,   'hewers of timber'   there are
indeed, <u>sp</u> but 'stave traders,' definitely not.

DOER   The barber's a shave trader, and any tinker you could
call a stove trader, <u>s</u> so now you sail   with staves
aboard,   why not call you   stave trader?

SIDEMAN   <u>sp</u> You're certainly fun to listen to. All right, all
right, what is it you want?

DOER   I'm a preacher called Layman Selfsame. I've come to
tell you how angry I am at the way you interrupted my
preaching.

SIDEMAN $\underline{s}$ In your own preaching you speak the truth, $\underline{sp}$
and in us there's nothing false.

        (Doer tosses robe toward Sideman.)

DOER   Well anyway, here's a robe that used to belong to
you. It shouldn't ever have left your boat, says he,

        (Doer picks up his skirts, mimes wading
      out to the boat and seizing the gunwale.)

dipping skirts   into the waves,   he grasps the gun-
wale   and arrests the craft.

SIDEMAN   Oho! Now I'm furious!   But nonetheless,   I respect
the cloth   and so won't hit you.   All this is that
girl's fault, cries he,

        (As though beating Child, he strikes his
      pole with his fan.)

and with an oar   savagely beats her.

DOER   Beaten, she makes no cry.   Why, she may be dead!

SIDEMAN   Why need she be dead?

        (Doer goes to Child and makes her stand.)

He pulls her to her feet, and see:

DOER $\underline{s}$ ropes bind her fast;
UTA
on-str

CHORUS   her mouth is gagged   with cotton wads,   and though
she weeps   her cries cannot escape.

        (In the spirit of comforting Child, Doer
      strikes excitement pose.)

MONDO
off-sp

DOER   Oh you poor thing! I'm going to take you back with
me. Don't you worry!

        (He sits Child down again and moves to
      center.)

MONDO
off-sp

SIDEMAN   All right, Layman Selfsame! Get out of my boat, fast!

DOER   Give her to me. You have the robe, my friend, so let me have the young lady.

SIDEMAN   I'd be glad to, but there's one problem.

DOER   What's that?

SIDEMAN   Well you see, we in the trade have a cardinal rule. And if you'd like to know what it is, it's that once we've bought someone, we can't ever give the person back. So I can't let you have her.

DOER   I understand perfectly. But we in my trade also have a cardinal and inflexible rule. And that is, that as long as we're unable to save a person whom we chance to find in dire distress, we can't go back to our cell. So, since your rule can't be broken, and mine can't be broken either, I'm not about to get out of your boat, even if you take me and the girl to the very depths of the North.

SIDEMAN   If you don't get out, I'll put you to torture.

DOER   Torture's an exercise in self-denial.

SIDEMAN   I'll have your life!

DOER   (firmly sitting himself down)   Take it. But I'm not getting out.

SIDEMAN   You say I can have your life, but you're not getting out?

DOER   That's right.

SIDEMAN   (muttering to himself)   This Layman Selfsame's really got me.

          (Grumbling so, Sideman gets out of boat and
          wades to shore, so to speak, by moving up to drums.
          Sideman's Second follows him.)

MONDO
off-sp

SIDEMAN   Well? Are you there?

SIDE SECOND   What do you want?

          (The pair face each other before drums.)

SIDEMAN   I want to know what we're going to do about this.

SIDE SECOND   As far as I'm concerned, we're going to have to give

her back. When you really think about it, it'd be

just terrible if the story got around that two slave

traders from up north came to Miyako and couldn't get

anyone, so they bought themselves a preacher called

Layman Selfsame and took <u>him</u> home instead. No, we've

got to give her back.

SIDEMAN   I quite agree. But I'd hate just to hand her back.

Let's have some fun with the preacher before we do it.

SIDE SECOND   An excellent idea.

          (They cover their right arm and shoulder
          again, and take fan in hand. Sideman's Second
          goes to sit near Sideman's spot. Sideman stands
          near main spot and addresses Doer.)

MONDO
off-sp

SIDEMAN   Quick now, out of the boat!

DOER   Well, well, Captain, you look pretty cheerful!

          (Doer stands and goes to main spot. Sideman
          sits at Sideman's spot. It is understood that they
          have reached the slave traders' own province.)

SIDEMAN   No, I'm not cheerful in the least. Anyway, my friend

here says that the first time he went to Miyako, he

heard about Layman Selfsame's dancing. He says for

you to do a dance.

DOER   Layman Selfsame has never danced in his life.

SIDEMAN   That's a lie. Last year when you preached as you just
              did, you woke up your drowsing audience by dancing
              right there on the High Seat. We heard about it even
              out here. So give us a dance.

DOER   Oh yes, that's Playful Words and Gorgeous Language;
              that's all right. If I do you a dance, then give me
              the young lady.

SIDEMAN   We'll see the dance first. If we like it, you can
              have the young lady.

SIDE SECOND   Here's a formal hat. Put it on and dance.

                      (Sideman's Second gives the hat, which he
                   himself has received from stagehand, to Doer.
                   Doer withdraws to stagehand's spot and puts it on,
                   then comes out to main spot.)

   MONDO
   off-sp

DOER   All things considered, they'll probably give the
              young lady back to me in the end. But they'll hate
              to just hand her over. I can see they're going to
              give Layman Selfsame a hard time, and try to embarrass
              him. (turning to Sideman) It's just too selfish of
              you!

SIDEMAN   Yes? What is it that's selfish?

   ISSEI
   off-str

DOER   (facing front)   Cape Kara in Shiga's   single pine,

CHORUS   all alone, ah,   what feels a man?

   CHU-NO-
   MAI

                      (With the last words above, Doer begins to
                   dance. He ends up at main spot as the text resumes.)

   MONDO
   off-sp

SIDEMAN   Your dance was too short. We didn't see enough.

DOER   Then I'll relate to you the origin of boats.

   KURI
   off-str

              Now then, concerning the origin of boats: their
              source is found in the Yellow Emperor's reign,

                  (He goes before drums and faces front.)

CHORUS   and their stream flows   from Kateki's pondering.

   SASHI
   off-str

DOER   For then there also lived a rebellious subject known
              as Shiyū.

CHORUS   His Majesty moved to crush him, but the waters of
              Ōgo intervened and he could not attack.

              (Below at 'icy gales,' Doer comes down
              front; at 'one leaf,' opens and looks down; at
              'spider,' sweeps right up to drums, then comes
              forward at little; at 'in the air,' looks up; at
              'single leaf,' glides down front and stamps beat;
              at 'perilously,' moves to mark post; at 'reached,'
              sweeps left up to drums; at 'why of course,' comes
              to center, does a leftright; at 'Yellow Emperor,'
              turns to right; at 'crushed,' faces front, then
              marks pause with a leftright and opens fan; at
              'therefore,' strikes fan high pose, then with full
              leftright comes down front; at 'since then too,'
              turns right up to main spot; at 'noble's craft,'
              goes to mark post, then, with fan displayed, sweeps
              left up to drums; at 'Dragon Prow,' marks end of
              dance with a leftright.)

   KUSE
   on-str

CHORUS   Among the Yellow Emperor's subjects   was a knight
              called Kateki. Once Kateki looked out   across his
              garden pond. Late fall was the season;   icy gales
              were scattering   the willow leaves.   One leaf
              floated   on the water   till a spider,   tossed up
              in the air,   dropped in too;   but riding   on that
              single leaf,   inch by inch,   most perilously
              before the blustering wind   the leaf drove on   and
              reached the shore.   Kateki, struck   by the
              spider's ploy,   thought, 'Why, of course!'   and

right away, purposefully, built a ship. The
Yellow Emperor went on board, rowed across the
water, and easily crushed Shiyū. Eighteen thousand
years ago, they say it was, when he brought peace
to his whole realm.

DOER   Therefore the graph for 'boat'

CHORUS   joins 'lord' to 'advance.' Moreover, since this
                    reign, the Son of Heaven's own ship is called
                    Dragon Barge, and a skiff is said to be 'one
                    leaf'; and since then too, a noble's craft
                    often is termed Swan-and-Dragon Prow.

    MONDO
    off-sp

SIDEMAN   I must say, it's really too good of you to eulogize
                    our boat as a 'Swan-and-Dragon Prow.' Anyhow, show
                    us, if you please, some sasara-rasping.

DOER   Then give me a piece of bamboo.

SIDEMAN   It just so happens that we've no bamboo on board.

DOER   Never mind.

    KATARI
    off-sp

                    Those hard, those painful practices the Buddha did
                    were to save all beings. The Layman, likewise, means
                    to save the young lady, even if he's to get ground to
                    bits in the process. Now, regarding the origin of
                    the sasara:

                         (Below, at 'onto his fan,' Doer opens fan;
                    at 'buzz buzz,' sweeps rosary over fan, then folds
                    fan; at 'rosary,' holds rosary before him and ex-
                    amines it, then grasps fan with pivot end pointing
                    away from him; at 'buzzing them,' does so; at
                    'ripples o,' stamps several beats as though playing
                    with waves; at 'Kara,' turns right while rubbing
                    rosary and fan together, and goes to main spot;
                    at 'not only that,' stamps several beats.)

There was in the Eastern Hills a certain monk who,
when pine needles fell on his fan, swept them off,
buzz buzz, with his rosary. Ever since, we've had
the sasara. This Layman, likewise, for rasp will
use his rosary, one hundred and eight beads,
and for bamboo his own fan's ribs, buzzing them
together. Here we are now on Shiga Coast

NORIJI
onori-str

CHORUS   and ripples o! and ripples o! Shiga Coast's
Cape Kara pine with top needles goes buzz buzz
like the sasara my rosary; not only that, but
my hands I rub now in abject prayer:

        (He faces Sideman, goes down on one knee
        and joins palms.)

I beg of you, please help me!

MONDO
off-str

SIDEMAN   Now I see you're rubbing your hands to me, I'll let
you have the girl. But while you're at it, beat the
waist drum for us.

        (Doer withdraws to stagehand spot, ties up
        his long, hanging sleeves, hangs the drum around
        his waist, takes a drumstick in each hand, and
        comes out to main spot.)

NORIJI
onori-str

CHORUS   Of old the drum was noise of waves

        (Doer dances, beating the drum. The
        dance is short, and in a manner which recalls the
        vigorous folk style.)

of old the drum was noise of waves rolling in
to pound the shore; when raincloud wandering
thunder god rumbles, bangs out his own sound,
rain comes falling pitter patter scrub bamboos
buzz rubbed so; ponds' hard ice cracks and

booms   the beaten drum,   <u>sasara</u> buzzing
playful words   are these and yet   voice of the
Dharma;   to Perfect Wisdom's   shore at last
borne,

        (Doer goes up to Child, has her precede
    him to main spot.)

UTA
on-str

from the boat   ratatat boom   he leads her out

        (Child exits. Doer opens toward front
    from main spot.)

and together   up to Miyako   they've gone   up to
Miyako   they've gone.

        (Doer faces side and stamps final beat.)

THE BLOCK
(Kinuta: a fourth-category play)

In The Block, breakdown of communication reaches a pathetic
nadir, and autumn feels very chill indeed. (This play is the clear
reverse of Takasago, in which communion is effortless and unfailing.)
The lady thinks her husband has abandoned her, whereas far away though
he is, he is only tremendously preoccupied. Thus she becomes es-
tranged even from her own self until she sinks into the pit of hell.
The fulling block she beats (see Glossary) reminds one of the expression, 'To beat one's head against a wall.' And yet, the wall is
illusory; it is only a misunderstanding. The lady is sure the tie
between husband and wife, which should last two lifetimes, has been
cut before even a single lifetime is over. In truth, though, her
husband is very constant. He doubtless had been hoping to go home
from one month to the next, and so had hardly written. It is only
when his wife dies of despair that he comprehends how little her need
for him has to do with his considerations of duty, and rushes home.
Once there he is able, because he really does love her, to call her
up from the grave and guide her phantom toward release.

This calling up and this guiding are related to some terms often
found in this volume: 'shadow,' or 'shade,' and 'raise,' or 'comfort.'
'Shadow' is ato, which basically means 'trace,' 'imprint,' 'mark.'
The word for 'raise' or 'comfort' is tomurau, and refers originally
to the very thing the husband does in The Block. That is, he twangs
his bowstring until, in the sound vortex created, the ato of the dead
appears. This technique for summoning spirits is associated with

shamans. A Buddhist monk would summon the _ato_ with the chanting of
sutras, and the husband here actually does both. Once the shadow is
present, it can be guided toward liberation.

The sutra used for guiding in The Block, as in Yorimasa, is the
famous Lotus Sutra, which teaches that each and every being, even the
weakest and most ignorant, can reach illumination. All that is needed
is to dedicate one's works, however insignificant, to the Buddha
rather than to oneself. This the girl in Layman Selfsame has already
done, and Komachi in Komachi on the Gravepost does it too in the end.
The lady of The Block makes this dedication after her death, for the
sound of the block she beats turns to a song of thanksgiving and
'opens into blossom heart of the Dharma.' The Lotus Sutra shows that
a Bodhisattva is one who has 'renounced full Buddhahood until all
beings be saved,' as Yuya puts it; and it is for the Bodhisattva to
help all beings make this dedication.

The Block alludes to one of the most famous passages of the
Lotus Sutra, the parable of the Burning Mansion. Some children are at
play in a ruinous mansion infested with dangerous creatures, and the
mansion is on fire. So intent are the children on their play, however,
that they notice nothing, and will not heed their father's urgent
calls to come out. Their father therefore has to lure them outside
with the promise of new toys: animal-drawn carts which shall be for
them to play with. These carts are really the vehicles of the Dharma;
while the Burning Mansion (called in Yuya the Mansion Ardent) is the
world of stifling ignorance and of clinging that burns like fire. It
is when a person turns his back on the Burning Mansion that communion

begins to be restored. While in the depths of hell, the lady of The Block is so cut off that even the block she beats makes no sound; a mirror, if she looked into one, would doubtless give back no reflection. It is her husband's concern that lets her spirit go free, just as in other plays it is the Sideman-monk's sympathy that brings comfort to a spirit.

Zeami, the author of The Block, said of it, 'No one in generations to come will grasp the flavor of a nō such as this.' It is hard to know exactly what he meant, but perhaps he had in mind the play's deeply sympathetic feeling for conjugal love; this gives The Block a tone rare in nō. Apart from the story of Sobu and the conventional situation of a husband long absent in Miyako, there are no known sources for The Block. Sobu, it should be noted, is Su Wu, a Chinese general who was taken prisoner by the Huns. His ardent loyalty, according to the original tale, was to the Emperor, not to his wife. This shift tells much about the Japanese concern with love.

NANORI- BUE	(Sideman enters, followed by Second. Side- man stands at main spot, facing front; Second, who wears the <u>tsure</u> mask, kneels on one knee behind him.)
NANORI off-sp	
SIDEMAN	I'm a squire from Ashiya in Kyushu. As I'm pressing a lawsuit on my own behalf, I'm residing here in the Capital. I thought I'd be in the Capital only a short while, but this year is already my third. Now I'm so worried about my home and family that I'm going to send the girl Yūgiri, my servant, whose name means Evening Mist, down to Ashiya.
	(He comes forward a little, then turns to face Second.)
MONDO off-sp	
	Come, Yūgiri, I'm so worried about my home and family that I'll have to send you down to Ashiya. Tell them I'll be down there for certain by the end of the year.
SECOND	Very well, sir, I'll be on my way immediately. You yourself will definitely arrive by the end of the year.
	(Sideman exits. Second stands and moves to main spot.)
AGEUTA on-w	
	For some time past travel wear day on day unfolds travel wear day on day unfolds till nightfall in endless inns dream follows dream on pillows borrowed
	(She takes a few steps to her right to show travel; then by the end of the passage is back in place and faces front.)
	noon and night I spend as in no time to Ashiya I've quickly come to Ashiya I've quickly come.

TSUKI-
ZERIFU
off-sp

> How happy I am! Hurrying along that way, I've come
> to Ashiya village. I must first announce my arrival.

> > (She goes to first pine and faces curtain.)

*
off-sp

> I beg your pardon! Is anyone at home? Please
> announce that Yūgiri has arrived from Miyako.

ASHIRAI-
DASHI

> > (Doer enters and stands at third pine,
> > facing front. She wears the <u>fukai</u> mask. Second,
> > meanwhile, retires to stagehand spot.)

SASHI
off-w

DOER

> Ah, in lovebird quilts   I suffer,   my husband's
> gone;   on turbot's pillow   sorrow   as waves
> sunder us.   Alas, estrangement's   mine to bear,
> yes, even as we two still live,   till memories
> throng: I weep the sound   of no forgetting,   my
> sleeves spill   tears' burning rain   so rarely,
> rarely clear

> > (She hides tears.)

> this heart of mine!

> > (Second has moved to first pine, where she
> > now stands facing Doer.)

MONDO
off-w*

SECOND

> <u>sp</u> Please make it known that Yūgiri has arrived!

> > (Doer lowers her head and turns to Second.)

DOER

> What? Yūgiri, you say? There's surely no need to
> be so formal. Please come in.

> > (Doer goes to sit before Chorus; Second
> > sits before drums.)

Well now, Yūgiri,   I'm delighted,   but quite
angry.   Perhaps indeed he's changed;   but if so,
why   did no wind   speed the news my way?

SECOND   <u>s</u> Madam, I was anxious to come as quickly as I could,
but his service   left me no time.   Unwillingly,
a full three years   I stayed in Miyako.

DOER   What?   You say it's unwillingly you lived in Miyako?

(Doer faces front.)

Think of that!   There in Miyako,   blossoming ever,
amidst a wealth   of consolations,   sorrow still
is the heart's own way!

SAGEUTA
on-w

CHORUS   How country life   palls, wearily   fall's soon
gone,   friends fade, grasses die;   his very vows
are broken now.

(She hides tears.)

What then to trust,   as life goes on?

AGEUTA
on-w

Were three years this fall   a dream   were three
years this fall   a dream . . . But no, the pain endures   all undispelled   memories   linger in me;
the old days change,   they've left no trace.
Yes, if this world   never lied,   how joyfully
I'd take his word!

(She lowers her head.)

Oh foolish heart!   Oh foolish, foolish trust!

(She suddenly looks up.)

MONDO
off-w*

DOER   <u>sp</u> Ah! Strange!   I hear a noise over there!   What
is it?

SECOND   That's the noise of someone in the village beating a
                fulling block.

DOER   Why, in my sorrow, an old tale's come back to mind.
                In Cathay, a man named Sobu was abandoned captive
                among the Huns. The wife and son he'd left behind
                at home longed for him, as he lay in uneasy rest
                through the cold nights; so they climbed a tall tower
                and beat a fulling block. Their love did apparently
                get through to him, for ten thousand leagues away
                Sobu, in his exile's sleep, heard that fulling block
                beaten in his far home. <u>s</u> I too shall ease my mind
                this dusk downcast   a figured robe   upon the block
                I'll beat,   yes, now I'll ease my mind!

SECOND   <u>sp</u> Alas, madam, beating the block's a task for humble
                folk! Bưt if it will ease your mind, I'll prepare a
                fulling block and bring it to you here.

MONO-GI-
ASHIRAI
                          (Doer withdraws to stagehand spot, while
                        Second sits before Chorus. Stagehand brings in the
                        fulling block and places it near Sideman's spot.
                        Doer removes outer garment from her right arm and
                        shoulder, then comes out to main spot.)

KAKEAI
off-w

DOER   Come, come, the block   we'll pound, she cries,
                where dearly loved I lay   on this our bed

SECOND   tears desolate   roll strait the mat

DOER   whence to tell abroad   my longing

                          (Second stands and goes to Sideman's spot;
                        Doer moves down front. Thus they sit on either
                        side of the block and gaze at it, absorbed.)

SECOND   now, Evening Mist   rises, draws near,   till lady
                and maid together

DOER   flail the block   of angry pain.

SHIDAI
on-w

CHORUS   Over the robe falls   voice of pines   over the robe

              falls   voice of pines;   night cold does wind

              as tidings bring.

                        (Both stand. Doer goes to main spot,
                    Second moves before Chorus.)

ISSEI
off-w

DOER   Scant the news from him,   a stranger,   it's to

              fall winds

CHORUS   this night

                        (Doer comes slightly forward.)

              I'll broadcast sorrow!

                        (She gazes into distance. Then, as Chorus
                    sings, she turns right and up to drums, where she
                    marks pause with a leftright.)

DOER   Village folk too,   far off,   come under that gaze:

CHORUS   the moon asks not   who claims the night.

SASHI
off-w

DOER   A striking time,   this fall eventide!

CHORUS   Stags' belling   quivers in the heart,   down mountain

              winds   invisible   which twig then   lets one leaf

              fall?

                        (She looks into sky.)

              Awful aloft   shines the full moon,   gleams on day

              lilies   at the eaves

DOER   where dewdrops hang,   gem-spangled blinds

CHORUS   the night through   shall I disclose   my agony.

                        (She lowers her head briefly.)

KAMI-NO-
EI
off-w

>'The palace clock points on high, wind shifts to the
>north;

DOER

>closeby a block beats fast, beats slow, the moon runs
>to the west.'

>>>(At mention of moon, she gazes into western
>>>sky. Now she looks around as each compass point
>>>comes up. At 'all clean,' she presses toward
>>>fulling block.)

UTA
on-w

CHORUS

>Sobu, exiled, sleeps   in the northlands,   while
>here is   the eastern sky;   come, you fall wind
>from the west,   blow all clean!   Now, pound this
>robe   of weave so thin!

>>>(She turns front again and advances slightly.
>>>At 'boughs,' she points around with fan to suggest
>>>the pine's branches; at 'traveling,' gazes at
>>>block; then points into distance with fan, stamps
>>>beat, gazes into eastern sky; at 'pining wind,'
>>>turns front again, then comes forward and opens;
>>>at 'this robe,' thrusts out left sleeve and gazes
>>>at it; at 'come near,' moves to mark post; at
>>>'thin vows,' sweeps left up to drums; at 'moonlight,'
>>>gazes up at sky toward front; at 'come, come,'
>>>turns to Second.)

AGEUTA
on-w

>Pine at the eaves   of his old home,   oh, have a
>heart!   In your boughs   let no storm-howl linger!
>Traveling   with this block's voice,   oh wind, blow
>to my Lord yonder!   Yet softly, softly,   pining
>wind,   lest my heart's desire   touch him there,
>and he see me . . .   Break not his dream!   Once
>it's broken,   why, this robe,   who'll come wear it?
>But if he comes,   for always   we'll cut the cloth
>anew.   Summer robe--   thin vows,   I hate him!

And may my Lord live   long the nights   when moonlight   keeps me from sleep;   come, come,
pound the robe!

> (Below, at 'surge between,' she comes down
> front; at 'paper,' turns right up to flute; at
> 'water,' advances to center as though gazing at
> edge of water; at 'froth,' opens fan, then strikes
> fan high pose; at 'eighth,' moves down front with
> a full leftright; at 'hue,' opens and looks into
> sky; then pointing low around her with fan, goes
> to mark post; then turns left, moves to side,
> listens; at 'lamentings,' hides tears and moves to
> block. Second then comes to Sideman's spot and
> both sit with block between them, as before; they
> strike the block turn by turn with their fans.)

KUSE
on-w

That Seventh Night   the lovers meet   a single time,
so thin,   till the River of Heaven's waves   surge
between them: a rapid tryst,   a fruitless
tossing craft there sails   with rudder paper-weak
tears fall, a dew   to make both sleeves   quite wilt
away!   Were they water weeds,   why then, o waves,
pound them close,   the froth, the foam.

DOER   Alas, dawn of the seventh day   of the seventh moon!

CHORUS   The eighth moon, ninth moon,   long, long nights,
oh thousand,   ten thousand voiced,   broadcast to
all pain!   Hue of the moon,   the windswept scene,
light glazed with rime: a time of anguish;   block's
beat,   night gales' howl,   lamentings, insect
noises   mingled fall   in dew, weeping   oh, oh, ho,
hah, ah, ah, ah,   they go, oh which   voice is the
block's?

> (She lowers her head. Second goes to mark
> post and sits facing her.)

MONDO
off-sp

SECOND   Madam, I must tell you that your husband will not be
back this fall.

KUDOKI
off-w

DOER   Ah, I hate him!   At least by year's end   said he,

lying,   while I pined here.   So it's true,

> (She covers her face with both hands.)

he's changed for good!

> (Second now goes behind Doer and puts both
> her hands against Doer's back, as though to give
> her strength.)

SAGEUTA
on-w

CHORUS   Think no such thing   urged my heart,   that now

breaks down.

> (Doer stands and moves toward bridgeway;
> Second follows, with her hands still on Doer's
> back. At 'finally,' Second stops near third pine
> and hides tears, while Doer continues on through
> curtain.)

AGEUTA
on-w

So cries die out   on fields gone sere   insect

voices   tangled grasses'   gay blossom heart   feels

wind turn mad   and on a sickbed   she sinks down

till finally   she's passed away   till finally

she's passed away.

> (Second exits. Stagehand now places the
> block down front. The Fool, who some time ago
> slipped in to sit at Fool's spot, rises and comes
> out to main spot.)

SHABERI
off-sp

FOOL   I'm the servant of a certain squire from Ashiya. My

master was away in the Capital for three years, on

account of a lawsuit, so he sent his maidservant,

Yūgiri, down to Ashiya, and had her announce that he'd

surely be home by the end of the year. My master's

wife felt the time drag by so that, in company with

Yūgiri, she diverted herself day and night by
beating a fulling block. Then another message came,
to say that my master wouldn't be back this year
after all. His wife soon died of grief and despair.
When my master heard this, he rushed back here in
great distress; but there's nothing he can do now,
except to offer up the block she beat until the last,
and to comfort her by raising her with the plucked
bowstring.

FURE
off-sp

I'm telling you this because he's ordered me to have
everyone in the village join in the rite. So please
be advised: you're all to be there!

> (Fool moves toward first pine, when Sideman
> enters, followed by Sideman's Second. Sideman is
> dressed for the rite, and carries a rosary.)

MONDO
off-sp

Ah, here's my master now.

> (He goes down on one knee before Sideman,
> who stops. Sideman's Second also goes down on
> one knee.)

I beg your pardon, sir, but I've made the announcement,
as you ordered.

SIDEMAN Did you leave the block just as it was?

FOOL Yes, sir, I left the block just as it was.

> (Sideman goes to sit before the block;
> Sideman's Second sits behind him and to his right
> and bows low, with palms pressed to floor. Fool
> retires to Fool's spot; he will slip out after the
> Doer's entrance.)

*
off-sp

SIDEMAN How cruel it is! Those three years away   hurt her
so   that my parting   from the wife I loved   proved
the very last!

AGEUTA
on-str*

> She's dead; I live still   and grief   eight
> thousandfold   the wild grasses   eight thousand-
> fold   the wild grasses   cover her,   yet from
> below, I hear,   there is a way   she may return
> one more time   to my good bow's high tip,   and
> we'll converse--oh, the pity of it!

>> (He hides tears.)

> $\underline{w}$ and we'll converse--oh, the pity of it!

>> (Sideman retires to Sideman's spot, and
>> Sideman's Second sits a little upstage of him. Doer
>> enters, carrying a staff and wearing now the deigan
>> mask. She stops at first pine, and faces front.)

DEHA

SHIMO-
NO-EI
off-w

DOER

> Three Shallows River: swallowed there I sank   as
> froth, alas,   down to misery!

>> (She lowers her head a moment, then comes
>> in to stand at main spot.)

KURI
off-w

> Grave-marker plums bloom gaily side by side, to
> display what spring this our world yields;

>> (She glances offstage, as if toward her own
>> grave.)

> lanterns lit to guide the wandering shade
> reveal the autumn moon, True Semblance.

KUDOKI
off-w

> Still, deep I lie in lustful karma: over-fond love
> smoked in me,   I knew no peace;   in sin so caught
> my tangled heart   strings twist hell fiends,
> Aborasetsu lash me ceaselessly,

>> (She turns angrily to Sideman.)

howl, beat on, beat!   my reward, the block.

        (She presses toward him.)

For hate

        (She turns front, hides tears; then,
weeping, comes forward slightly.)

NORIJI
onori-w

reaps me the fruit   of wrongful clinging

CHORUS   reaps me the fruit   of wrongful clinging;   anguished

tears   fall to the block

        (She leans on staff with both hands,
stares vacantly ahead. At 'breast,' she lowers
head weakly; at 'choked,' looks up in agony; at
'no voice,' listens intently; at 'pining wind,'
looks toward bridgeway; then starts forward, but
instead weakly retreats, dropps staff, sits, covers
ears with hands.)

and tears no more,   turn fire;   in smoke and flame

my breast smothers,   choked, I shriek,   but no

voice!   Soundless the block,   nor do I hear

pining wind,   only cursing fiends,   oh terror!

        (Now she stands, opens toward front, stamps
beat. At 'on and on,' she goes to mark post, then
sweeps left up to center; at 'wheel,' turns left
up to drums, as though wandering; at 'never,' advances toward center; at 'wretched,' claps palms
together; at 'anger,' hides tears; at second
'anger,' moves, weeping, toward main spot; at
'one way,' stops, turns, advances toward Sideman;
at 'shame,' lowers head and faces front; at 'two
lives,' looks up and stares at Sideman; at 'trust,'
turns right, pointing with fan around her, and
moves to main spot; then turns and moves toward
Sideman as far as center; at 'all lies,' strikes
right knee with fan, then points with fan at Sideman; at 'fibber,' faces front; at 'who'd say,'
moves down front with a full leftright; at 'in
fact,' turns right and up to flute; at 'across,'
moves to center while gazing into distance; at
'deep,' turns intently to Sideman; then, pointing
at him with fan, goes before him, kneels on one
knee, stares; as Sideman sees her coming, he salutes

her with joined palms. At 'at least,' Doer
strikes stage once with fan, points left hand
accusingly at Sideman and then, suddenly, weeps.)

DAN-UTA
on-w

As sheep walk or   colt flicks past crack   as sheep

walk or   colt flicks past crack,   on and on revolve

the Six Ways;   unless the cart   that's cause and

fruit   wheel out the Burning Mansion's gate,   it

shall turn   round and round,   yet never quit   the

sea of birth-and-death!   Oh wretched,   oh dismal

life!

DOER

My anger grows,   as creeper vine leaves,   one way
only

CHORUS

my anger grows,   as creeper vine leaves,   one way

only,   clinging in my face shows,   oh, shame, shame!

Husband of mine,   it's two lives   you promised me,

yet my fond trust   we'd last   a thousand ages,

till the seas   wash Pine Mountain   turned out empty

waves dash high hopes now! All lies, it was! But

was your heart then so?   The fibber-bird   they call

crow,   he has a heart;   but you--   who'd say you're

true?   Grasses and trees   know their times,   birds

and beasts   have real feeling!   In fact, Sobu,   the

one I spoke of,   tied his letter   to a wild goose

southward bound,   and across ten thousand leagues

it got through;   no doubt because   the bond was

deep,   the love not shallow.   Oh husband,   with you

gone,   through night's cold   your robe   I beat and

beat: how can it be   that really,   or at least in

dream,   you knew nothing?   Ah, I hate you!

(With head still lowered, she turns front,
stands, goes to mark post; then, at 'phantom,'
sweeps left up to center; at 'see then,' advances
slightly, gazing at block; at 'short,' turns right
and up to main spot; then, facing front, joins
palms; at second 'seed,' turns to side and stamps
final beat.)

KIRI
on-w

Now by the might   of the Lotus Sutra   now by the
might   of the Lotus Sutra   the phantom's way   runs
brightly traced   to Buddhahood.   See then: the
voice of the block   a short while struck   opens into
blossom heart   of the Dharma,   has turned seed
of illumination   has turned seed   of illumination.

CRAB BITES YAMABUSHI
(Kani yamabushi)

(To music, Yamabushi enters. He is followed by Porter, who carries a big, conical kasa
hat tied to a pole. Porter sits at back of stage,
while Yamabushi stands at main spot, facing back
of stage.)

YAMABUSHI   Ōmine and over   to Kazuraki   Ōmine and over   to

Kazuraki! I'm going back to the mountain I call

home.

(He faces front.)

I'm a Yamabushi from Mount Haguro in the land of

Dewa, and I'm just down from the Peak. I'm done with

Ōmine and Kazuraki, and right now I'm on my way home.

You there! Porter!

(He goes to Sideman's spot. Porter stands.)

PORTER   I'm here, sir.

(He goes to main spot.)

YAMABUSHI   I'm going home, so you come with me.

PORTER   By all means, sir.

(Yamabushi starts walking. Porter follows
behind.)

YAMABUSHI   Now, now, come along, come along!

PORTER   I'm coming, sir, I'm coming!

YAMABUSHI   Well, those hard, agonizing practices I did back
there are really something, aren't they!

PORTER   As you say, sir, they're really something.

YAMABUSHI   And what do people have to say about my powers?

PORTER   They're calling you a Fudō incarnate, sir, a veritable
Fudō incarnate.

YAMABUSHI   If they're calling me a Fudō incarnate, they must be
                 calling you a Seitaka or a Kongara!

PORTER   That's right, sir, I'm sure they are.

                          (Having gone once around stage, Yamabushi
                          stops at Sideman's spot. Porter, meanwhile, is at
                          main spot.)

YAMABUSHI   Well! Before you know it, we've come out on a big
                 bog. What's this bog called, I wonder?

PORTER   Why yes, sir, what could this bog be called? I've no
                 idea.

YAMABUSHI   I have it! This must be Crab Bog in Ōmi.

PORTER   That's right, sir, it does look like Crab Bog.

YAMABUSHI   Say! It's clouding up, and it sounds as though the
                 mountains yonder are rumbling. We'd better not stay
                 too long around here. Let's hurry on closer to a
                 village.

PORTER   That'd be fine, sir.

                          (Yamabushi starts walking toward bridgeway.
                          Porter moves so as to fall in step behind him.)

YAMABUSHI   Now, now, come along, come along!

PORTER   I'm coming sir, I'm coming!

YAMABUSHI   Damn, I hope nothing happens on the way to the village.
                 I don't like the atmosphere around here.

PORTER   You're right, sir, the atmosphere around here isn't
                 very nice.

                          (Crab spirit sidles in, wearing the
                          kentoku mask. He holds his arms out, elbows
                          angled, and his fingers form pincers. Yamabushi
                          runs into him on bridgeway.)

YAMABUSHI   Yeeow! Yeeow! Yeeow! Get over here! Get over
                 here!

                          (He escapes to Sideman's spot.)

PORTER   Very good, sir! Very good, sir!

> (He follows, stands in front of where no
> Chorus sits. Crab comes to main spot.)

YAMABUSHI   Some monster's loose over there!

PORTER   You're right, sir, something or other's loose over there!

YAMABUSHI   There isn't another path, by any chance?

PORTER   No, sir, not a one.

YAMABUSHI   Hold on there, hold on there. A man like me runs into a monster at Crab Bog, and doesn't speak to it? Why, I'd never live that down. Come on, I'll try talking to it.

PORTER   But sir, you shouldn't get too close to it!

YAMABUSHI   Just you _try_ and get me close to it!

> (He steps forward.)

Ahoy, you out there! What are you?

CRAB   I, sirrah, am the spirit of one whose two eyes are in the heavens, whose one shell touches not the ground, whose two big legs and eight little legs move him lightly right and left.

YAMABUSHI   His two eyes are in the heavens, his one shell touches not the ground, his two big legs and eight little legs move him right and left, right and left . . . Hmm. Then it has to be the spirit of a crab.

PORTER   You're right, sir, it does seem to be the spirit of a crab.

YAMABUSHI   Damn! Why'd that crab spirit have to pop out right here?

CRAB   Because you're so stuck up about your powers. I've shown up to block you.

YAMABUSHI   Well! Did you hear that?

PORTER   I heard it, sir, I most certainly did.

YAMABUSHI   He's a crab, and he thinks he's going to block my
              powers? Why, that's absolutely ridiculous!

PORTER   Oh, sir, a nasty character, sir! One like that, let
              me just smash his shell with this vajra staff here, and
              I'll make soup out of him for our camp tonight.

YAMABUSHI   No, no, you'd better not!

PORTER   No, no, sir, it's no trouble at all!

                    (Porter slips hat off pole and strikes
              offensive pose.)

              You nasty character, you! Let me smash that shell of
              yours with this staff! Hey! Hey! Yaah!

                    (Various attacking movements accompany these
              last sounds. Porter tries to strike Crab. Crab
              skips aside, and, before drums, seizes Porter's
              left ear in his right pincer.)

              Owowowowowow!

                    (He holds himself up with the staff.)

YAMABUSHI   What happened? What happened?

PORTER   Sir, the crab's got his pincer clamped onto my ear!

YAMABUSHI   Now look what you've done! That's just why I told
              you not to!

PORTER   Oh please, pray and make him let go of me!

YAMABUSHI   Right you are. I'll just hit him with one little
              prayer, and he'll drop you.

                    (At Sideman's spot, he faces front.)

              A yamabushi, you see, is called yamabushi because it's
              in the yama, the mountains, that he bushi, that he
              makes his lair.

                    (He turns to Porter.)

How was that? Just fine?

PORTER No, sir, not just fine at all. I think he's going to rip my ear off.

(Yamabushi turns front again.)

YAMABUSHI Now, this hat I wear, it's called a tokin. You take a strip of cloth, dye it black, quick make pleats all round, put it on your head, and you've got a tokin. And this chaplet: this is no irataka chaplet with the big, flat beads.

(He exhibits his chaplet a moment.)

This one is made of plain plant seeds. Pray one little prayer with this chaplet, and anything can happen.

(He turns to face Crab, holds chaplet out and rubs beads vigorously together while mumbling a nonsense spell.)

Boron boro boron boro boron boro.

PORTER Owwww! Owwww! Oh please, please, sir, stop!

YAMABUSHI What's the matter?

PORTER The more you pray, sir, the harder he pinches.

YAMABUSHI What? The more I pray, the harder he pinches?

PORTER Absolutely.

YAMABUSHI All right, all right. Then this time I'll pray him to death.

PORTER Oh sir, do please do that!

YAMABUSHI Right you are!

(He addresses Crab.)

However evil this crab, I'll put all my faith in Fudō's rope and pray one prayer--then any miracle can happen!

(He rubs beads together.)

Boron boro boron boro. 'Under the bridge, the
irises, who planted them, the irises? Tug away, but
they won't break, cut away, but they won't cut . . .'
Boron boro boron boro boron boro.

> (His prayer consists of a late twelfth-
> century popular song. Now, Crab sidles up to
> him, still dragging Porter, and catches Yamabushi's
> right ear with his left pincer. Flute starts a
> dramatic shagiri solo. All three are lined up
> before drums. After they have danced to the flute,
> Crab drops both flat on their faces and skitters
> out, sideways.)

YAMABUSHI   Owwww! Owwww!

> (He gets up.)

Damn, damn, damn! Where'd that crab go?

> (Porter scrambles to his feet.)

PORTER   Yonder, sir!

YAMABUSHI   Follow that crab! I'll get him yet! I'll get him yet!

PORTER   I'll get him yet! I'll get him yet!

> (Both exit in pursuit of Crab.)

THE WATCHMAN'S MIRROR
(Nomori: a demon play)

Thorough restoration of communion and wholeness comes very con-
vincingly in The Watchman's Mirror. The season once again is spring.
Up from the nethermost gulf the demon comes, gives the Sideman the
mirror of all-knowledge, and disappears. The circle is complete, and
the next play can only be a god play once more. 'God' and 'demon' are
closely related, and The Golden Tablet, a very old god play, is like a
demon play with the polarity reversed.

Mirrors often appear in nō. The full moon aloft is mirrored in
all waters, showing that the one truth shines from within every being;
Pining Wind recoils from her image reflected in the sea; the lady of
The Well Cradle sees her own face mirrored as her lover's when she
looks into a well. When one includes in this theme the encounter between mirror image opposites, then Nightbird is as much a mirror play
as The Watchman's Mirror, and Granny Mountains is a vast discourse on
the subject. Granny Mountains, especially, makes it crystal clear that
'Back links it is that lift one high' is really the very same theme.

As war can be seen as the most manly of all pursuits, and love
as the most womanly, warrior plays and woman plays are often not far
apart. Perhaps woman plays come after warrior plays because woman is
intrinsically further from enlightenment than man (so the Buddhist
feeling on the subject does go); or perhaps love is more truly central
in human life. In either case, the play remains a vision or a dream
that is definitely external to the Sideman. In obsession or miscellaneous plays, the Sideman may already be much more involved, but the

play's last-minute ending is still not completely satisfying. In the
case of a demon play, however, it is the Sideman himself in whom the
circle is completed. (In <u>Granny Mountains</u>, the Second is the real
Spectator, and the Sideman is only her appendage; the Sideman in nō is
never a woman.)

In <u>The Watchman's Mirror</u>, what the Sideman sees in the mirror
is really himself, that most difficult of all demons to face. In
particular, it is himself reversed, or the Buddha reversed. That is
why the demon is a demon, and why the Sideman speaks of reversing the
mirror to the Dharma-Savor. However, once the Sideman takes the mirror
in both hands and gazes into it, both he and the demon have to vanish,
and the play is over. The mirror is now a sphere of light centered
on man's heart. It no longer reflects opposing images. Buddha (or
god) and demon are one, and the pit and the heavens are one space.

The Emperor's presence in this play, and in <u>Nightbird</u>, tells
much. Long ago, the Doer says, he met His Majesty on Kasuga plain and
'basked in the Imperial gaze, though unworthy.' But when he appears
in his true form--it was his true form 'then' as well as 'now'--it is
the Sideman's gaze that he basks in. Long ago the Emperor found his
lost white hawk, a powerfully symbolic bird, by looking deep into the
pond; and now the Sideman sees the universe and himself in the 'real'
Watchman's Mirror. Thus the Sideman and the Emperor must be at
bottom the same person: he who surveys the universe at a glance from
the top of the central mountain. Indeed, one name for the Imperial
Palace is Ōuchi-yama, translated in <u>The Golden Tablet</u> as 'Inmost Peak.'

The whole meaning of <u>The Watchman's Mirror</u> is suggested by its

first lines. The 'sewn-in gem' mentioned there is from a parable in
the Lotus Sutra in which a man gives his friend a priceless gem. The
friend, however, is fast asleep, so the giver sews the gem into his
clothes. When the friend wakes up, he does not realize that he is
immeasurably wealthy, and goes his way. This gem is the perfectly
luminous nature which, like the moon's reflection, is in all beings.
And yet, as beings are not awake, and are kept in darkness by ignorance,
they do not know they have it. The Sideman knows in theory that it
is there, but it is only at the end of the play that he makes it truly
his own.

The term 'watchman's mirror,' nomori no kagami, is known in
poetry, and explanations of it are given in several collections of
remarks on poetry that Zeami, who wrote the play, undoubtedly knew.
However, there never seems to have been any particular pond by that
name.

SHIDAI

(A mound, represented by a light structure, stands before drums. Sideman enters and stops at main spot, facing upstage; he turns to face front after singing opening verse.)

SHIDAI
on-str

SIDEMAN

Mosses soak dew   into these sleeves   mosses soak dew   into these sleeves   where lurks   the hidden gem.

NANORI
off-sp

You have before you a roving monk from Yusurugi in the land of Noto. Being bound for Ōmine and Kazuraki, I'm just now hurrying toward Yamato.

AGEUTA
on-str

These days my   inn Kashima plain,   headrest of grass   inn Kashima plain,   headrest of grass, with Rat abed   and up with Tiger,   sleep, as now, ever   quickly caught

(He takes a few steps to show travel, and is back in place by second 'have I come.')

by moonlight   on westward, yes   to slow-trailed Yamato land   have I come   Yamato land   have I come.

TSUKI-
ZERIFU
off-sp

Hurrying along that way, I've come to the village of Kasuga in the land of Yamato. First, I believe I'll ask someone about the sights to be seen near here.

(He retires to Sideman's spot.
Doer enters, leaning on a staff and wearing the asakura-jō mask.)

ISSEI

ISSEI
off-str

DOER

Out he comes,   who on Kasuga plain   watches signal fires,   to see, and look!   very soon now   we shall pick greens!

NANORI-
ZASHI
off-str

        The old man   who comes before you   here on Kasuga
        plain   lives out his years   visiting hill,   touching
        at hamlet: Old Man   Watchman of the Plain   is he.

SASHI
off-str

        Oh blessing!   The hues of spring,   in mercy's works
        complete,   mantle Mikasa hill;   the winds of fall,
        Fivefold Sole Consciousness   visit Kasuga village.
        Straight indeed the vow   of the gods' will   most
        careful   do I come and go,   each step I tread
        building high,   praise be to them,   the summit of
        my age.

SAGEUTA
on-str

        Cathay itself has heard tell   of this temple-shrine,
        so glorious its name!   In the old days

AGEUTA
on-str

        Nakamaru   in the old days   Nakamaru,   missing this
        our Sunrise Land,   sang 'Back to Heaven's Plain
        turn I my gaze . . .'   to praise   o'er Mikasa
        hill   the rising moon!   Yonder,   the moon of
        Ming!   Here, at glorious Nara,   beauty of a   mild
        day in spring   beauty of a   mild day in spring!

MONDO
off-sp

SIDEMAN   (stands)   I beg your pardon, old man, but I have a
        question to ask you.

DOER   What is it you wish to ask?

SIDEMAN   Are you from here?

DOER   Yes I am.   I'm the watchman of Kasuga plain.

SIDEMAN   If you're the watchman, then tell me, please: is this

pond here, intriguing as it looks, actually famous
in some way?

> (Both look toward the pond, which is in
> imagination located down front.)

DOER   This is the very pond that's called Watchman's Mirror.

SIDEMAN   How curious! And why is it called Watchman's Mirror?

DOER   It's called Watchman's Mirror because a watchman like
              me sees himself reflected in it from morning to night.
              But the real Watchman's Mirror, I hear, is one a demon
              owned long ago.

SIDEMAN   You say it's actually a demon's mirror that's called
              the Watchman's Mirror? What do you mean?

DOER   Once upon a time, they say, there was a demon who
              lived on this plain. By day he was a man, and watched
              the plain, but by night he was a demon and lived in
              the mound here. So as the mirror belonged to a demon
              who watched the plain, it's called the Watchman's
              Mirror.

        KAKEAI
        off-str

SIDEMAN   A fascinating tale!   Then, some will say   it's what
              the demon owned   who watched the plain   that's
              called   the Watchman's Mirror;

DOER   and some, that since   the watchman sees   himself
              reflected there,   the pond as well   takes the name
              Watchman's Mirror.

SIDEMAN   Both tales will stand

DOER $\underline{w}$ for now as long ago   the watchman's title's

SIDEMAN   quite unchanged.

> (Doer presses toward Sideman, then moves
> down front to gaze into pond.)

DOER   Then look!

AGEUTA
on-w

CHORUS   I move close, and   indeed the watchman's   water mirror   indeed the watchman's   water mirror reflects this form   more and more   age ripples in crease the clear pond,   alas!

(He steps backward to center.)

How I do long   to see myself   as I was then!

(Now he turns right and up to main spot; at 'that's' he faces Sideman; at end of speech, he faces front.)

Yes, yearn one may,   but fruitlessly!   In the old days   the watchman   owned the mirror--that's a tale   of times now gone   that's a tale   of times now gone.

MONDO
off-sp

SIDEMAN   May I say something? Does the poem, 'Sparrow hawk finder, Watchman's Mirror . . .' refer also to this pond?

DOER   Yes, it does.

(He sits at center.)

It's a story told about this pond. I'll relate it to you.

SIDEMAN   Please do.

DOER   Once upon a time, while hunting on this plain, His Majesty lost his hawk. High and low he searched, and while so doing came upon a watchman of the plain. 'Old man,' he asked, 'do you know where my hawk has gone?' Then the old man said, 'Yes, it's at the bottom of this pond you'll find your hawk.'

(He half-rises. At 'stepping,' he
suddenly stands and comes down front, holding
staff before him, and gazes into pond.)

'How could my hawk be at the bottom of this pond?'
exclaimed the hunter, stepping up to look: $\underline{str}$ and
sure enough,   there far below

AGEUTA
on-str

CHORUS   he was, or seemed,   white speckled hawk

(He steps backward to center, touching
staff to ground; at 'closer,' gazes forward as it
were into the trees, then moves down front and
looks into water.)

he was, or seemed,   white speckled hawk;   a closer
look   and yes, it proved   a reflection   in the
water   underneath a tree!

(He steps backward again· to center, looks
up while resting both hands on staff; then goes
to face front from main spot.)

It's up there   the hawk was perched!

AGEUTA
on-w

Yes, the song   'Sparrow hawk'   yes, the song
'Sparrow hawk   finder,   Watchman's Mirror,   would
you were mine!   Unseen I'd see   does she love me
or no,'

(He turns to Sideman.)

was made   because of   the hawk's reflection.

(He comes down to mark post, then sweeps
wide left up to main spot.)

An age truly splendid   and rich the hawking   on
Kasuga plain   the Watchman   of Signal Fires   met
his good Lord,   basked in the Imperial gaze,   though
unworthy;   in old age now   it all comes back:

(He faces Sideman, then sits at center
facing front.)

as I talk,   the flooding tears!   as I talk,   the
flooding tears!

       (He hides weeping.)

RONGI
on-w

CHORUS   Indeed a tale   of ages past.   Now I've heard it
show me, pray,   the real Watchman's Mirror!

DOER   Unthinkable request!   A mirror, that,   for demons--
how should you look within?

CHORUS   Why then,   I'd learn the place   the mirror lies
on Kasuga plain

DOER   Watchman am I;

CHORUS   the mirror, why

       (Doer turns to Sideman.)

DOER   should it not be mine?

CHORUS   you wonder, yes!   That mirror   a demon owns: one
look   would terrify you.

       (Doer stands, moves swiftly to main spot.)

The real mirror   you would see   but there's no way-
ward the white hawk

       (He advances toward Sideman, glaring.)

once seen   in the water mirror: look in <u>there</u>
says he,

       (He goes beside mound, opens toward front,
then enters mound.)

and slips   into the mound   and slips   into the
mound.

MONDO
KATARI

       The Fool, who for some time past has been
sitting at Fool's spot, now stands and moves to
main spot. He introduces himself as a man from
Nara out on a journey, then sees Sideman and calls

to him. Sideman says he has a question, so Fool comes to center. There he tells the stories of the Watchman's Mirror and of the hawk, adding nothing new. He says the old man Sideman saw just now must have been the Watchman's phantom, and urges Sideman to raise him with prayers. Then he withdraws to Fool's spot, to slip out after Doer's entrance. Sideman now stands, as music resumes, and advances toward the mound.)

*
off-str

SIDEMAN   That I witness   such a wonder   no doubt is thanks

to the power   of my practice;   so, confident,

before the mound   where the demon lives   I've

prayed my guts to dust.

(He drops to one knee, takes his rosary in hand, and joins his palms.)

If that Dharma-might   I've built up   year in, year

out   by my work   is real,   then bring out   your

magic mirror,   demon,   show me wonders!

(He rubs his rosary beads together vigorously, producing a rhythmic buzzing, and repeats several times this formula:)

All hail, my refuge in the Buddha!

DEHA   (Sideman now retires to Sideman's spot. Powerful, dramatic music is played. Doer chants from within mound.)

*
str

DOER   <u>off</u> Oh wondrous blessing!   <u>onori</u> Heaven and earth it

moves, touches god and demon;

CHORUS   <u>off</u> soil and sand,   mountains, rivers,   plants and

trees,

DOER   all,   as the One Buddha   ripens to the Way   are

drawn on to   the Dharma-Savor;

(Doer emerges from rear of mound and faces front from main spot. He now wears the <u>kobeshimi</u> mask, and holds before him a great, round mirror.)

NORIJI
onori-str

CHORUS   Demon outrages   clear, spotless   the Watchman's
                Mirror   stands displayed!

KAKEAI
off-str

SIDEMAN   Oh terror!   Glittering with sparked fires   the
                mirror's face   throws back the light   of demon
                eyes!   No, I cannot face it!

                          (Doer lowers mirror and hastens back beside
                     mound, where he stops.)

DOER   If you're afraid,   then I must go,   the demon says
                and starts into the mound.

SIDEMAN   Wait, demon!   Just a moment!   Deep the night still,
                the pre-dawn bell . . .

DOER   Tiger's the hour,   the Watchman's Mirror

SIDEMAN   reverse, I pray,   to the Dharma-Savor,   cries he,

DOER   the rosary

SIDEMAN   furiously buzzing.

                          (Sideman stands and goes on rubbing rosary.
                     Doer meanwhile frequently stamps beat. At 'reck-
                     less,' Doer moves to mark post, displays mirror;
                     then turns left up to flute; at 'Kongara,' moves
                     to center, displays mirror left and right; then
                     turns right up to main spot; at 'Diamond,' opens
                     toward front; at 'East,' stamps several beats.)

CHU-
NORIJI
on-str

CHORUS   T'ai Summit's   clouds have I trod   T'ai Summit's
                clouds have I trod,   year-long have   built up
                power   a thousand days and more,   often reckless
                of my life,   with no time   to pick fruit,   draw
                water.   One, Kongara,   two, Seitaka,   three,
                Kurikara,   Seven Mighty,   Eight Mighty   Diamond
                Minions;

*
off-str

in the East

MAI-
BATARAKI (Doer moves to mark post, sweeps left up
to drums, comes down front, turns right and ends
up at main spot. As text resumes, he moves down
front again, holding mirror before him; at 'South,'
back to main spot, where he holds mirror toward
curtain and peers within; at 'Heavens,' to mark
post holding mirror horizontal, drops to one knee
and peers within; at 'Earth,' stands, holds mirror
aloft and horizontal, stamps beat; at 'Crystal,'
opens toward front, displays mirror; at 'lightness,'
steps backward to main spot, drops to one knee,
strikes stage twice with fan, displays mirror to
Sideman while pointing into it with fan; then
stands and moves to center.)

NORIJI
onori-str

DOER in the East, Gōsanze the Bright King, Queller of
the Three Ages shows in the mirror;

CHORUS now to reflect South, West, and North:

DOER all points immaculate brightly shine

CHORUS the Heavens now,

DOER the No-Thought, the No Non-Thought Heavens themselves, to their confines;

CHORUS now to mirror the vast Earth:

DOER first, the realm of Hell,

CHORUS first, Hell it shows then changes to the Crystal
Mirror Eight Feet Broad: lightness or weight of
sins, the sinners' screams beat on beat the
iron rods raining blows, all is revealed.

 (At center, he drops to one knee and thus,
half-kneeling, advances toward Sideman and gives
him the mirror; then he stands and stamps beat;
at 'away,' stamps several beats; at 'homeward,'
goes to mark post, pivots on himself, stamps; at
'rumbles,' sweeps left up to main spot, stamps;
at 'gulf,' drops to one knee.)

The Clear Mirror   this, a treasure   that puts
straight   all demon outrages!   Away!   It's to
Hell   I'm homeward bound!   says he,   stamping
till earth rumbles,   stamping till earth gapes,
split   to the nethermost   gulf of Hell   has he
gone in.

      (He stands, stamps final beat.)

GLOSSARY

bardo. Chūu, the period between death and rebirth, generally said to last seven times seven days.

Blue Sea Waves. Seigaiha, a bugaku dance.

bowstring resin. Kusune, resin cooked with oil and made into a coating that strengthened a bowstring. The presence of a bow in the house promoted harmony.

Chōnō. Fujiwara Chōnō, or Nagatō, a mid-Heian period poet. No text which includes this quotation has survived.

crystal mirror. The mirror of Emma, king of the underworld. It reflects the soul's good and evil deeds.

Diamond Minions. Kongō dōji. The Eight Great Diamond Youths are eight followers of Fudō.

First Emperor. Ch'in Shih-huang-ti, the emperor who unified China for the first time in 221 B.C. Once when he was out hunting he took shelter from the rain under a small pine. The pine instantly grew tall and thick, at which the First Emperor was so pleased that he gave the pine the title 'Marquis.'

Five Blocks. Goshō, the five obstacles in the way of enlightenment: passions, karma, being alive, dharmas, knowledge.

Five Ways. The Six Ways, minus Ashuras.

Fugen. In Sanskrit, Samantabhadra.

fulling block. A fulling block is used in the process of thickening woolen cloth by heating and pressing. A kinuta, however, is a block on which cloth, most likely silk and certainly not wool, is beaten in order to clean it and to give it lustre.

Fun'ya no Yasuhide. A ninth-century courtier and poet. Like Komachi herself, he was one of the 'Six Immortals of Poetry' of the period.

gargoyle. Literally, a 'demon tile,' the tile used to terminate the ridge of a roof. It ends in a disk bearing the grinning features of a demon.

Home to the Palace. Genjōraku, a bugaku dance.

Hori Inlet. A busy artificial harbor near the mouth of the Yodo River, mentioned here because of the association of ideas with 'boats throng, contending. . . .' Hori Inlet seems also to have been a proverbial place to drown.

Iki Pine. A pine said to have been planted on the shore in Kyushu, facing Korea, when Empress Jingu (r. A.D. 201-269) sailed on her expedition of conquest to Korea.

Jambudvīpa. The continent on which men live, to the south of Mount Sumeru. Embu in Japanese.

Kajiwara Kagetoki. Died in 1200. A general under Minamoto no Yoritomo. At Watanabe, the harbor whence Yoshitsune sailed to Yashima in pursuit of the Taira, Kagetoki urged that the Minamoto fleet be equipped with sculling oars at the bow as well as at the stern. This was so that the ships could retreat in case of danger as well as advance. Yoshitsune violently disagreed with Kagetoki's attitude, and vowed he would have no such 'reverse oars' on his own ship.

kalavinka. In Japanese, karyōbinga: a bird that sings in paradise.

Kasuga Plain. A plain near Nara. The name evokes ancient memories of the imperial house. Kasuga plain was famous in poetry as a place to pick the first green shoots of spring.

Kongara. With Seitaka, an attendant of Fudō.

Kurikara. The black dragon who is sometimes seen coiled around Fudō's sword, and who is the fluid aspect of Fudō.

lady-pine. Hime-matsu, a species of pine.

Lady Sayo. When her husband sailed from Matsura (Pinebeach) as an imperial envoy to China and Korea, she climbed a hill and waved her scarf until the ship disappeared. Several Man'yōshu poems concern her.

laurel (hall). The katsura, a kind of laurel tree, is said to grow on the moon.

Live-Oak Plain. Aoki-ga-hara, the actual place of origin of the God of Sumiyoshi, in eastern Kyushu.

Lone Cloud. Another name for the Purple Cloud on which Amida rides as he comes to greet the souls of the dying.

lovebird quilts. Literally, mandarin-duck quilts: paired mandarin ducks are a symbol of conjugal love.

Ming. Not the Ming Dynasty, but one of the provinces of the T'ang empire.

Mount T'ai. A sacred mountain in China, conventionally associated with such sacred Japanese mountains as Ōmine or Mount Hiei.

Nakamaru. Usually pronounced Nakamaro. Abe no Nakamaro, a poet, went in 716 as a student to T'ang China. He was never able to return to Japan.

no-thought, no non-thought heavens. The highest of the heavens in the three realms.

ox. The hour of the Ox is the time period centering very roughly on 3 A.M. It is a time when spirits both good and bad are abroad.

Pinefest. Matsubayashi, a kind of party popular in the fourteenth and fifteenth centuries. It involved singing and dancing, and was held in the first moon of the year, either at home or in a pine grove.

pristine zone. Mizugaki, the fence around the inner precincts of a shrine.

Rainbow Skirts and Cloak of Wings. A T'ang Chinese dance of Central Asian origin. The T'ang emperor Hsüan-tsung is also said to have transmitted it after personally visiting the moon (thanks to the Taoist arts) and witnessing the dance of the maidens there.

Rakuyō. A poetic name for Miyako; actually the Japanese reading of the name of the ancient Chinese capital city of Lo-yang.

rat. The hour of the Rat is very roughly midnight.

River of Three Fords. Sanzu no kawa, another name for Mitsuse-gawa, Three Shallows River. This river surrounds the underworld and is crossed by three fords: shallow for the good, middling for the average, and deep for the wicked soul.

sasara. A folk musical instrument, a kind of rasp.

Seishi. In Sanskrit, Mahāsthāmaprāpta.

Seitaka. With Kongara, an attendant of Fudō.

Shaka Nyorai. The Japanese for Shakyamuni Tathāgata. Shakyamuni is the name of the historical Buddha. Tathāgata, Nyorai, is a title referring to his enlightened condition. It means something like 'He Who Comes Just As He Is.'

six sense roots. Rokkon, the six senses. These are the five particular senses, plus consciousness. To each corresponds one of the six dusts: forms, sounds, smells, tastes, touch sensations, and dharmas

Ten Thousand Years. Manzairaku, a bugaku dance.

Thousand Autumns. Senshūraku, a gagaku dance.

three realms. Sangai, the three realms which comprise all existence: desire, form, and the formless.

Three Treasures. The Buddha, the Dharma, and the Samgha (the community of monks).

tiger. The time period centering roughly on 4 A.M.

tokin. A tiny hat that yamabushi wear perched on their heads. Yamabushi costumes can be very elaborate.

true phrase perfectly contained. Jissō muro: truth whole, unfragmented, and undistorted. A roundness and fullness like that of an ocean or the full moon.

Tsukushi. An old name for Kyushu. 'Of mystic fires' (shiranu hi) is a stock epithet for Tsukushi, but the exact meaning of the term is not known.

turbot's pillow. Hiboku no makura. The hiboku, or hirame, is a flat-fish like a flounder. It became in China and in Japan a symbol of conjugal love. The turbot is a fish of this type.

twelve dependent links. Jūni innen, the twelve-fold chain of causation distinguished by the Buddha as causing and perpetuating the cycle of birth and death.

Vergogne. The Forest of Vergogne is Hazukashi no mori, a forest not far from Miyako. Hazukashi also means 'ashamed.' This use of the French word 'vergogne' is an attempt to translate the meaning without rendering the translation flavorless.

willow comb. Tsuge no kushi. Tsuge means 'boxwood,' but is written with the characters 'yellow' and 'willow.' The image of a willow fits very well with that of a breaking wave.

Yakushi. Bhaishajya-guru, the Buddha of Healing, whose lapis lazuli blue (or deep green) paradise is in the east.

yellowbark. Kihada, a shrub belonging to the rue family. The bark was used for stomach ailments and for burns.

CORNELL EAST ASIA SERIES

For information on ordering the preceding publications and videotapes, please contact:

CORNELL EAST ASIA SERIES
East Asia Program
Cornell University
140 Uris Hall
Ithaca, NY 14853-7601
Phone: (607) 255-6222